The WISHBONE Boys

The Tear Away, The Bloodstains, The Wishbone

About the Author

Tim Card, filmmaker, author

Tim is a member of the Screen Actors Guild (SAG-AFTRA), and is an established filmmaker and stuntman. His ambition for film came at an early age.

Tim was inspired by Burt Reynolds, Clint Eastwood, Robert Shaw, Sergio Leone and Hal Needham. At 18, he started working professionally as a stuntman on the TV series "The Dukes of Hazzard."

Tim continued his career as an actor/stuntman doing feature films such as "Under Siege," "Stroker Ace," "Sharky's Machine" and "Six Pack." He has also produced and directed commercial videos.

Tim studied drama at the University of South Alabama and attended the Burt Reynolds Dinner Theater and various filmmaking and stunt workshops.

Tim's lifelong dream was to produce feature films, which he has achieved. He has worked with talents such as Burt Reynolds, Steven Seagal, Ned Beatty, Tommy Lee Jones, Dom DeLuise and stuntman/director Hal Needham. Fueled by his passion for Alabama football, Tim has produced a film on the greatest era in Alabama football history entitled "The Wishbone Boys," so named for the highly successful wishbone offense.

"Tim Card"

"The aspect that drew my passion about this particular project was the wishbone offense at Alabama. It was in my heart when I was a small child. I knew that there was something special about it. I decided that I was going to do a project honoring it somehow. That's when it just hit me (The Wishbone Boys). The next thing that I had to do was talk to Coach Mal Moore. When I first approached Coach Moore about this era, he said, "Those were magic times." I told him that I wanted to produce a documentary about the wishbone offense at Alabama. He was quite enthusiastic about the idea and wanted to help in any way that he could. Because of his efforts and sincere interest in the project, this is dedicated to Coach Mal Moore with honor and respect."

The Wishbone Boys

Tim Card

Robert Wray

Film Systems International. Inc.

Library of Congress Cataloging-in-Publication Data Card, Alabama Football, Bear Bryant, The Wishbone Boys/ Robert T. Card. - 1st ed. 1. Sports 2. College Football I. Title.

Published in the United States of America.

Dedication

This project is dedicated to Coach Mal M. Moore 1939-2013, without whose encouragement it would have never come to fruition.

Mal M. Moore (December 19, 1939 – March 30, 2013)

As a player, coach, and director of athletics, Moore was part of ten national championship football teams. In May 2012, he was inducted into the Alabama Sports Hall of Fame.

As a scholarship player from 1958–62, Moore played as a career backup quarterback for Coach Bryant, behind Pat Trammell and subsequently Joe Namath.

He began as Bryant's graduate assistant in 1964, then as defensive backfield coach for six seasons, before becoming quarterback's coach and serving as the Tide's offensive coordinator starting in 1975.

He was instrumental in the installation and implementation of the wishbone offense prior to the 1971 season. The move to the wishbone led to an unprecedented decade of success for Bryant and the Crimson Tide.

Moore directed more than $240 million of capital improvements to University of Alabama athletic facilities.

Moore's dedication to and love of the University of Alabama was recognized on March 28, 2007, when, as a permanent tribute to his lifelong contribution to The University of Alabama, the Board of Trustees of The University of Alabama officially dedicated the facility formerly known as The Football Building as the Mal M. Moore Athletic Facility.

In 2011, he was elected to the State of Alabama Sports Hall of Fame for his accomplishments as a coach and an administrator. After the completion of the 2011-12 academic and athletic seasons, Moore was named the winner of the John L. Toner Award, given to the nation's best athletic director.

"This is the beginning of a new day. God has given me this day to use as I will. I can waste it or use it for good.

What I do today is very important because I am exchanging a day of my life for it. When tomorrow comes, this day will be gone forever, leaving something in its place I have traded for it. I want it to be a gain, not a loss – good not evil. Success, not failure, in order that I shall not regret the price I paid for it."

– Heartsill Wilson

Table of Contents

Acknowledgments

I am very grateful to the many individuals who reviewed my draft manuscript and provided their feedback. I want to thank my friends Jim Harper, Rob Alpha, John Prestridge, Jeff Candeto and the men who realized this dream and played the game. Of course, I thank my parents B. Jefferies Card, Peggy Nance, Mabel J. Card. Also the individuals who gave generously of their time and experience. I thank all of them, especially Executive Producer Buffy Donlon (Class of 1973), Co-producer A.P. Steadham, Associate Producer Bob Wray, Michelle Ryan, Fred Lee Davis (Class of 1941), Fred Lee Davis, Jr. (Class of 1965), Lee Pruitt Barksdale, Director of the Paul W. Bryant Museum Ken Gaddy, Heather Moore Cook, Deirien Howard, Shaun Leftwich, Joe Cicio, Angeline Herron, Steve Sprayberry, Jimmy Sharpe and Kirk McNair, Rachel Deloach, Hannah Chalker Goodin.

Foreword

This book has significance to every Alabama fan as it documents a critical period in her football history. It presents in detail the effort and success of the coaches and players.

At the end of the 1970 season when Alabama was struggling with six-five seasons we ended up playing Oklahoma in the Bluebonnet Bowl in Houston. Oklahoma had switched to the wishbone during the season after playing Texas and it was a very simple wishbone. That game ended up 24-24. The next day we were flying back to Tuscaloosa. Normally, I would sitting about in the middle of the plane and Coach Bryant would sit up front. But on this trip he sat right next to me. He pulled out a legal pad and started drawing up the wishbone. We went through spring practice with Billy Sexton at quarterback and we were using a pro set drop-back game. Coach invited Darell Royal to speak at the Alabama coaching clinic that they held at the end of July. Coach Royal brought his offensive coordinator Emory Bellard with him. He was the person who brought the wishbone up to the college game from the high school. Before the clinic ended Darrell Royal told Emory to stay in Tuscaloosa a few days and work with the Alabama coaches. They stayed at the Holiday Inn near the interstate with a chalkboard and a projector and Emory showed all the clips. They learned the wishbone in a couple of days.

Mal Moore had been a defensive coach, but Coach Bryant had him move to offense. That was a pretty tough move for him, especially with a new offense. Coach Bryant always said a good coach can coach anything. The coaches were to keep it quiet. They thought they would only try it for a while and then go back to what they were doing. Coach Bryant wasn't the kind of guy to lose his guts and he said we're going to sink or swim with the wishbone. They worked it and ended up changing quarterbacks to get to get someone who could run and throw - that was Terry Davis. Mal told me later that he was a magician. That's what it took, because Alabama, unlike a lot of other teams ran the wishbone formation. Rather than just call plays they were going to actually be reading the defense end - whether they were running right or left. They would not block him if he went outside. They gave it to the fullback if they went inside or they would pitch to the tailback. It's split-second decisions and good ball handling. I remember my boss, Charley Thorton, who was Sports Information Director at the time said, “I don’t know whether to be more excited about the offense or the defense.”

We were practicing on Monday night and a bunch of students had started at a pep rally five blocks away from the practice field and the pep rally had moved to the practice field. Coach Bryant yelled down from his tower to go open the gate and let the students in. That famous Friday night game against Southern California turned out to be what a lot of people say was the most important game in Alabama football history. Alabama upset Southern Cal 17 to 10. It was a tremendous game. On the Eastern Time Zone a lot of people would not even know the score. The game was probably over at midnight back there. I remember going up to the coach’s suite and Coach John David Crow said after the statistics were read, “I'm a hell of a coach”. I think the important thing about that game was that it really energized Coach Bryant because he had been on the verge of leaving. Although this was halfway through his career, he ended up winning nine SEC championships and three national championships.

That game was held on Friday night so it didn't get the play on Saturday that it would have normally received and it wasn't televised. It was a hard game to find out about or a follow but by Sunday it was big news across the country. It made the Sports Illustrated cover that year and they said “Bama’s Back”, so it was a huge game in media coverage.

In 1977 we went back to Los Angeles to play Southern Cal again and of course we were well-established at that point as one of the best teams in the country. We went out on a Thursday so we had a lot of time. I was up in Coach Bryant's suite and while we were going over the details of the game, the phone rang. I answered the phone and it was the operator. She said I know I'm not supposed to be calling up there, but Mr. John Wayne called and wants Coach Bryant to please call him. I said I'll certainly give him the message. I was thinking I'm going to hear one side of this conversation but Coach Bryant said I don't have his number here so I'll call him when I get back to the office so unfortunately I didn't get to hear that conversation.

I want to say it was a delight to work with Coach Bryant. He was one of the hardest working people I've ever known. Everybody around him was a hard worker, but not because they were intimidated or scared, but because they didn't want to disappoint him. I never wanted him to call my office and not have me be there. I remember a friend saying he couldn't wait to get up in the morning and go to work. That was the truth. It was a delight to see the second half of his era materialized behind the wishbone. I have to put in a word for Mal Moore. He really took advantage of that offense much more than anyone else.

No one had a sophisticated wishbone like Alabama. You can put that right back on Coach Bryant because he said what you're looking for in football is to get one-on-one coverage on your receivers. We figured out real quick that you had that almost every play with the wishbone. Alabama really incorporated the passing game into the wishbone and had records for years for most yards per completion. When they threw it you always had the defense running to the line of scrimmage to try and protect against those runs. You got big plays out of the passing game. We had good receivers like Wayne Wheeler, Ozzie Newsome and Joey Jones so that so that was an important part of it and Coach Bryant loved it.

We went to play Arkansas at the end of the 1979 season in the Sugar Bowl to win a second straight national championship. We moved our half backs up into the slots rather than back behind the fullback. It was the exactly the same offense, but now the lead tailback was starting from the slide and the other half back was sweeping wide around. This ABC reporter came in and asked what the heck is Alabama doing with this new offense? I said it's the same offense but the half-backs are just set up differently. It showed that Coach Bryant was always tinkering to improve it.

When we played Virginia Tech in 1973, we had four guys rush for over a hundred yards - one of the first times that it has ever been done in NCAA history. I remember in the 1979 Sugar Bowl against Penn State that Mal apologized to Steadman for not playing him more and Steadman said, "coach I don't blame you". Steadman was a lot faster than most people thought.

Terry Davis was the best Wishbone quarterback. It was the hardest for him because he didn't have any breaking in. He came right in. Mal would say I'm thinking about this play and he would draw it up on the board and stand back and think about it. Davis would say, yeah that might work for a yard. Mal said all he wanted to do was run the triple-option.

A lot of guys did not want to work in the wishbone because they wouldn't get to play enough to get an opportunity to play in the NFL. We weren't teaching pass blocking. Coach Bryant said by the time I get them where they can learn to pass block, it's time for them to leave so we don't even teach it anymore. From that standpoint you were at a disadvantage recruiting offense players because you weren't getting them ready for the NFL. But the ace in the hole was you get to play for Coach Bryant and that helped us keep the wishbone going. We had great players. At one of the reunions they were showing a highlight film and somebody stood up in the back and said, did the defense play in any games that year? It was the truth. On Sundays the coaches would go over the game and the offensive reel would be big and the defensive reel would be very small. The defensive coaches were through in about an hour because the offense kept the ball all day and the defense got off the field very quick.

When we were getting ready for that famous Southern Cal game (1971) we switched to the wishbone in practice but really no one knew about it. Coach Bryant was very media-friendly. Although we would let reporters watch practice and talk to Coach Bryant, I would have to say you can watch but you can't write anything about it. I remember telling one reporter that you can't write anything about the wishbone and he said, what is the wishbone? When the reporters would come in, we would practice the old offensive strategy not the wishbone because it was so secretive. We had a situation as we were getting ready to go to Southern California. We thought our radio team, John Forney, play by play and Doug Layton, the color guy they were completely in the dark. That Monday we brought them in and took them up to the meeting room. Coach Sharpe and Mal Moore explained to them that we would be running the wishbone. They drew it up and gave them a little lesson about it but they were sworn to secrecy. John told me later that even in the pregame they did not mention the wishbone. Of course in the game we went right down the field and scored with the wishbone. Before the game he had met with the Southern Cal radio team and we said we're doing the same old thing. After that play the Los Angeles team gave him a one figured salute so it was a well-kept secret. Because of the schooling they had gotten, they were already to announce a great game which they always did. Back in those days, you weren't on TV every week the way that you are today. You were on TV maybe once or twice a year during the regular season so the radio broadcast was really important. This was a Friday night game and not on TV and you know the people back in Alabama were really tuned in and they were as surprised as anybody hearing about Alabama going to the wishbone.

Back then radio was the way to go and they were so good. John and Doug really knew football and that was a real Plus for Alabama.

Well you couldn't do it the same way we did. You couldn't trust the reporters that covered Alabama now, not that they're not honorable people but there are so many of them. A lot of them are doing internet stuff and many of them don't have that same degree of integrity that we had back then. Of course there were a lot fewer reporters back then and they appreciated what Coach Bryant did for them. It would never happen today. If Nick Saban was putting in some kind of secret plan, there wouldn't be any reporters out there.

Kirk McNair

Introduction

1971 was a year of tension and uncertainty. The country was rocked by the disclosure in Washington of the Pentagon Papers showing duplicity by former President Johnson regarding Vietnam. Closer to home, Alabamians were proud of the City of Birmingham's designation as an "All-America City," hopefully the beginning of the racial healing so sorely needed across the state.

But, in Tuscaloosa, some things never change. Speculation of the Crimson Tide's prospects for the 1971 football season was underway, and no one was happy, least of all Coach Paul "Bear" Bryant.

The 1970 season had begun poorly with a very sound whipping by USC in Birmingham and ended with a 6-5 record, including losses to archrival Auburn and a tie with Oklahoma in the Bluebonnet Bowl. After putting together three National Championship teams in '61, '64 and '65, and an undefeated team in '66, the Alabama fan base from across the state was clamoring for more of the same.

After back-to-back 6-5 seasons, they were asking, "What happened?" Championships had become a way of life, and the expectations were nothing less.

Thus opens the era of the "Wishbone Boys"— so named after the offensive football strategy that became legend and ushered in three more National Championships in '73, '78 and '79 and set the standard for all future teams to measure themselves against.

The wishbone era at the University of Alabama was the single most motivating influence to thousands of Alabamians of the 1970s, a time of hardship, monetary devaluation and more Washington scandals. But at least they had one thing — a coach that had "never been nothin' but a winner" and his belief that he could teach and motivate young men to believe in themselves.

So begins the film "The Wishbone Boys"— a film about believing with the right strategy, the right motivation and belief in themselves that a team with a less-than-stellar record could capture the imagination of all of NCAA football fans. To this day, this magical era conjures up larger-than-life stories of the teams that won more than just football games, but the hearts of fans.

This film accurately traces the creation of the wishbone offense by Emory Bellard, assistant to Coach Darrell Royal, how it was secretly co-opted by Coach Bryant and reconstituted in a form that could be secretly taught to the Alabama team without playbooks or written information.

This film includes interviews of the coaches and players of the era that were the "boots on the ground." It includes never-before-revealed information about the strategies, plays, players and coaches who were sworn to secrecy before the first game of the '71 season. It is all brought back to life through game footage and sideline commentary with all the intrigue and excitement of a best seller.

The timeline of "The Wishbone Boys" spans late 1970-1983. With the help from the Paul W. Bryant Museum and the blessings of the University of Alabama Athletic Department A-Club, the filmmaker Tim Card has had the opportunity to interview dozens of players and coaches from the era. His love for this project and encouragement from many people who lived and breathed the wishbone offense has made "The Wishbone Boys" film projected to be "Nothin' but a Winner!"

Forty-nine percent of all profits from this film will be donated equally to the University of Alabama A-Club foundation and the Big Oak Ranches. It is dedicated to Coach Mal Moore, without whose encouragement this film would never have come to fruition.

In the late spring of '71, after two disastrous previous seasons, Coach Bryant call a meeting of the offensive coaching staff to reveal the new plan: the wishbone offense. Under a veil of secrecy, Coaches Jimmy Sharpe and Mal Moore fly to Austin, Texas to meet with Darrell Royal and observe the wishbone offense during the last week of spring practice at the University of Texas – a most valuable trip that led to 116 victories, 11 bowl games and three national championships.

They brought back the plan – no playbook and never written down. At the end of July, Coach Bryant finally told all the plan for total change to the offense. When the Texas coaches Alabama for a high school event, Texas coach Emory Bellard met with Coach Bryant and his assistant coaches.

When the second semester of summer school practice began, everyone was sworn to secrecy. When the press attended practice, the team ran the old offense. The element of surprise was paramount.

What is the wishbone?

The wishbone is an offensive formation designed to run a triple-option with a lead blocker. The purpose of the option is to eliminate one defender without blocking him. Ideally, the defender must make a choice to eliminate one of two offensive players. This is a double option. This option offensive scheme forces a defender to choose one of two offensive players who can advance the ball and then allows the other offensive player to carry the ball, making whatever choice the defender made the "wrong" choice. Because of this aspect of the defensive player taking himself out of the play by his choice, the offensive player that would otherwise block that defensive player can now block a different defender, placing severe pressure on the defense to cover the dive, the quarterback run, the pitch or the pass to a receiver.

The triple-option eliminates two defenders without blocking them. This frees two offensive linemen to block different defenders, usually inside defenders. This isolates the dive key and the pitch key for the quarterback to "read" and should leave only the safety and the cornerback to cover the end, who maybe running a deep pass route.

To run a triple option with a lead blocker is the reason for the wishbone formation. It is the extra blocker concept that drives the success of the wishbone. The cornerback must cover the outside receiver. The safety must support the run defense and covers the pitch back. The defensive end typically attacks the quarterback and a defensive tackle is assigned the fullback dive. These assignments must be made before the play begins and that totals eight defensive players to both sides of the ball.

However, the offense now has linemen that can be released to block other defenders. The play is designed to handle five defenders on either side of the ball. The defender least able to affect the play - the offside cornerback or deep safety, is not blocked by design. The offensive linemen, now free to block inside, can block the first down lineman to the playside and the first linebacker to the playside. Emory Bellard once said, "If the threat of the fullback can be applied to the defense, the offense is sound." Then, the lead back principle takes over. The lead back can block the defensive end or the safety and there is then a “one-on-none” possibility for the offensive player with the ball. In order to stop this attack, the defense must defeat blocks or flow defenders to the playside.

This makes the wishbone a complete offense. The offense expects to get a one-on-none in the running game and a one-on-one in the open space with the passing game. The safety, who must support the run and also defend against the pass, is under tremendous pressure in this attack. The basic wishbone triple option play accounts for every defender on the field. Every defender is threatened before the basic play begins. There is an invitation to overplay or compensate on the basic play and overplaying or making a misstep on the basic play leaves the defense open for counters that leave no one to make up for the mistake.

The wishbone has the quarterback taking the snap from under center, with a fullback close behind him, and two halfbacks further back, one slightly to the left, and the other slightly to the right. The alignment of the four backs makes an inverted Y, or "wishbone", shape. There is typically one wide receiver and one tight end, but sometimes two wide receivers, or two tight ends.

The quarterback is a running back who can throw. He must also have an aptitude for the option and the decision making that lies within the play design as well as durability.

The fullback is required to be able to handle a physical pounding because he is frequently hit without having the ball; he must also be quick with excellent stamina, and be a good blocker.

The wishbone was designed to facilitate a running, option offense. It allows the quarterback to easily run the triple option to either side of the line. The quarterback first reads the defensive tackle or linebacker who is unblocked. As he reads the tackle/linebacker, he rides the ball in the fullback's gut. This is the "belly" play. There was a certain terminology that Mal Moore used in describing the offense. It was "reach and flow" - reach back to the full-back and flow with him to the line. Go down and make a decision.

If the defensive tackle/linebacker looks to tackle the fullback, the quarterback pulls the ball out and runs down the line to his next option read, usually the defensive end/outside linebacker. If the end/linebacker looks to tackle the quarterback, the ball is pitched to the trailing halfback. The lead halfback is a lead blocker usually looking to block the outside defensive player, a safety or corner.

"The quarterback and the fullback have to have that feel. The full-back can't be looking at the quarterback. Anytime you would get a fumble somebody wasn't doing their job." – Billy Jackson

"Penn State had two tackles that could read the "belly" play, we called it. If the fullback doesn't get the ball it presents problems for the wishbone because you're trying to read that tackle and get him out of the way. We couldn't do that with Bruce Clark and Matt Millen because they were on both sides of the ball. If a team had one good tackle, you could just go to the other side, but they had two that were very agile and very strong." – Major Olgilvie

Wishbone Origins

It was Charles Cason, a Fort Worth football coach, who first modified the classic 'T' formation. Emory Bellard learned about Cason's tactics while coaching at a high school nearby.

Earlier in his career Bellard saw a similar approach implemented by former Detroit Lions guard Ox Emerson, a head coach near Corpus Christi. Trying to avoid the frequent pounding of his offensive line, Emerson moved one of the starting guards into the backfield, enabling him to get a running start at the opposing defensive line. Bellard served as Emerson's assistant at that time. During his high school coaching career in the late '50s and early '60s, Bellard adopted the basic approaches of Cason and Emerson, and won championships using a wishbone-like option offense.

In 1967 Bellard was hired by Darrell Royal and became offensive coordinator a year later. After watching Texas A&M—running Gene Stallings' option offense—beat Bear Bryant's Alabama team in the 1968 Cotton Bowl Classic, Royal instructed Bellard to design a new three-man back-field triple option offense. Bellard tried to merge his old high school tactics with Stallings' triple option out of the Slot-I formation.

Introducing the new offensive scheme at the beginning of the 1968 season, *Houston Chronicle* sportswriter Mickey Herskowitz stated it looked like a "pulley bone", while Royal agreed but changed the name to "wishbone". Royal quickly embraced the idea of the wishbone, which proved to be a wise choice: Texas won 30 straight games, leading to two national championships using the formation.

In 1971 Royal showed the offense to Bear Bryant, who was so enamored with it that he installed it at Alabama complete with his own touches. Bellard later left Texas and – using the wishbone – guided Texas A&M and Mississippi State to bowl game appearances in the late 1970s.

The wishbone's reliance on execution and discipline, along with its ability to eat up the play clock, made it a favorite of programs that routinely play opponents with superior size and speed.

Coach Jimmy Sharpe – 1963-1973

"What do you remember about Coach saying that he wanted to install a whole new offense called the wishbone?"

I remember that and every coach that was in that meeting remembers it a little bit differently. I remember that he called us all together and said that he had just come back from visiting with Darrell Royal and decided that he would go to the wishbone offense and wanted to get our opinion. The majority of coaches there said, we can win with what we've been doing, so you haven't convinced me to do anything different. He said, "We're going to the wishbone and if any of you can't go along with that I'll help you find a job". But he gave us a chance to speak our mind.

"What was your opinion about the wishbone at that time?"

I knew a little bit about it, having watched it. It's a different perspective and the next thing that happened after that meeting was vitally important to the success that we had. It was an unknown. It's one thing to draw a play on the board, but to know how to teach it bothered us. Mal Moore and I talked at length after that meeting. Coach Bryant told us that Coach Royal was coming in August and would go over everything. Our players reported two weeks after that and we were very concerned. I went in and told him about our concerns. We had finished our spring practice so I and the other offensive coaches needed to understand how to coach it - the drills and those things. He said that he would think about it. He came down to our office about an hour later and said to Mal Moore and I that the school plane would be at the airport in two hours and we were going to Austin. Texas had only two days left in the spring practice. So we flew to Austin and their coaching staff was most gracious. We were interested in watching their drills and listening to their coaching points, all the little things and being able to teach the wishbone.

"When you got back you only had 3 weeks to teach the wishbone, is that right?"

We went to Austin at the end of their spring practice so that was probably about May. Our players don't report until August. We had a little time to discuss with the other offensive coaches what we saw. We were able to come up with our version of drills. We felt that we could teach this. We asked Coach Bryant if we could we bring in the centers, the full-backs and the quarterbacks for that second session of summer school. He let us do that so we were able to have some sessions. We were able to teach our first understanding to those young guys so we had a little bit of teaching sessions prior to the team coming in.

"What was the idea behind the secrecy and keeping the practices hush hush?"

The year before Southern Cal had beat us pretty soundly and we knew that they had better talent man to man than we did. So we did not want them to know what we were doing, so the element of surprise would be to our advantage. There was a coming together of the players and the team. There were a few press members that Coach Bryant took into his confidence. Everybody bought into it. I remember the week before the game, we had been practicing and nobody knew what we were doing. Coach would make us run the other formations. We had a former player that was that was coaching at a junior college in California not far from Southern Cal. I called him and I said, "Dennis I want you to drive by and look at their practice and tell me if they're working on the wishbone". For three days in a row he called me back and said all they're working on is split backs. That was right up until the week before we went so the surprise did make a difference, but our players were ready.

“I heard from some of the other players that Coach Bryant said you were going to either sink or swim so what kind of risk is that?”

When I was a freshman back in 1958, Alabama had not won many games. Coach Bryant told a group of freshmen, “I've seen your work and I like what I see. I've got a plan, if you'll listen to me, if you'll work hard in 4 years you'll be national champions”. In 1961 we won the national championship. A lot of us knew that when he said we're going to sink or swim, the odds that we were going to swim and swim well.

“What was going through your mind during that Southern Cal game?”

The excitement was incredible. We were anticipating what they would do. I remember the first play and I have a picture somewhere of our offensive line coming off the ball on that first play. You can literally see that they are in their second step and the defensive players from Southern Cal still had their hands on the ground. They're not reacting. It was that kind of exhilaration and we were not going to be denied.

“As a coach how pivotal was that game in the next decade of Alabama football?”

The record speaks for itself - the 71, 72 and 73 seasons and then on and on. The neat thing about the wishbone was that it brought people together. They were really sold on what we were trying to do and it was a neat thing to be a part of.

"What were you and Coach Bryant thinking after you won that game?"

There was never any doubt in his mind, so he never approached a game thinking that he couldn't win the game. He knew that if we could get an advantage we would win. That's what football is all about - getting a little extra advantage. Our defense could hold on and we could win and that's what happened. Anyone that saw the game knows that in the second half Southern Cal began to make great strides in stopping our offense. We had already done the damage and we had our points on the board. The defense rose to the occasion and slammed the door and we went home the victors. When we flew in to Alabama, there were more people at the airport then at the stadium. It was an incredible beginning to the wishbone years.

"What about the quarterback preparation?"

Some people really have a knack of understanding. They have good athletic ability, but it's more than ability. It's a feel. There's certain mechanics that you have. When we were in Texas, one of the former quarterbacks told Mal some of the intricacies that nobody would know - that coach Royal didn't know. For example, how to move your wrist, how to do this and that. So we worked on techniques and the details so much that we knew in every game we would have an advantage.

"How did the 71 and 72 seasons affect your success in the 73 season?"

The season was a great one and we wound up expecting to win like just like when I was a freshman. Coach Bryant said we would win a National Championship and that's all any of us ever wanted. Going into the 73 season Coach Bryant told us that we're going to be on TV for these particular games. Those things were stacked in our favor. "If you will just do your job" he would say. He had the ability to lay out a big picture so real you could taste it. There was an excitement about the 73 season. It was just a good time.

"Do you think the wishbone could be run successfully in today's game?"

I don't think that the wishbone is shutdown per se, but some of the tactics that coaches use in running it, like the philosophies of the triple option part are run very effectively today. Part of what Auburn and Oregon run is the read option. That's the part of the wishbone that they use. They've just taken folks and split them out wide but it's the same thing. At the beginning of the wishbone the offensive linemen could not use their hands. They were confined to blocking with their shoulders. During those early years we perfected techniques for our smaller lineman. They were technique freaks. It was very effective. By using our techniques and the triple option concept we could take a great defensive player and turn him into a guy that's thinking about his assignment. That's what the wishbone did. That's what the triple option or the read-option is doing in professional football today. You have a great linebacker who saying to himself - do I get the quarterback or the back? That was the real concept - you were attacking people and not having to block. If you don't have to block, then you've got some other players that can outnumber the defense and that's what we were trying to do get an advantage.

"What was your favorite thing about coaching the wishbone?"

The offensive line. I had great joy in seeing the success that they had against bigger players. There's a lot of the techniques that we developed at Alabama out of necessity that are used across the country today. It's hard to overcome the joy that you see in the players like Steve Sprayberry or John Hannah. The winning will take care of itself. if you have folks that achieve their goals.

“Is there a game in your career that sticks out in your mind?”

I was talking to Wayne Wheeler about this. We all know about the opening play against Tennessee - that touchdown pass. In my 20 something years of coaching you draw a lot of x's and o's. You think about a lot of plays but very seldom do you see a play that you thought about or dreamed about that is 100% successful. When I think about successful plays, I think about that play. The reason is that in our breaking down leading up to that game. For five games in a row we had opened the game with a quick-hit to the fullback carrying the ball up the middle. The reason we did that is that we wanted to see what the defensive responsibilities were. Who had the quarterback, who had support, because that would define how we called our plays. We did it for five games in a row. Coach Bryant always like to run the ball to see what they were doing first. We said let's put in a new play. Let's run a pass and hit wheeler on the post. We put the game plan up on the board in Coach Bryant's office. Mal and I would leave it and Coach Bryant would look at it. We said we want to start with this play and coach said, “what?” We told him why and he said leave it up there. We never said anything else about it. Later in the week he said, “I'm considering starting with that play”. So we got the okay to start with that play. Wayne Wheeler gets told that we're running the play prior to the game. During our warm-up, I told the offense what the first play was going to be. Buddy Brown was the offensive right tackle and Tennessee had an All-American super defensive tackle playing against him. I said guys were going to score on the 1st play if we sell the run. I said Buddy you've got to come off and butt that defensive tackle and knock him to his knees. Buddy Brown comes off the ball and butts the defensive tackle and knocks him to his knees. That is the most perfect play that I can think about during the wishbone years. We drew it up and it happened to perfection, but that doesn't happen much.

Terry Davis – Quarterback - 1970-1972

"How did you get recruited to Alabama?"

I guess it was a little strange. I grew up in south Louisiana and I always wanted to go to LSU. That was my goal, to play for LSU and sometime during my junior year in high school Alabama sent a brochure. I thought a little bit about it, but not much more. And then Jeff Rogers showed up in town and came by to see me. I had never seen Alabama play football. In those days there was only one game a week on TV and usually it would be LSU. But after a little bit of visiting with Coach Rogers and thinking about Alabama, Namath, Kenny Stabler and some of the greats who played there, it began to get more interesting. Basically they just out recruited LSU in my senior year. The Alabama recruiters were in my little town at least once a week. They just showed a lot more interest so I think I made a good decision.

"What did you hear about Coach Bryant?"

It was scary and awesome. You hear so many stories about him, about how tough he was and he was tough, but he was a gentleman. I remember when I was up there playing. It was my first game against South Carolina. After the game he took six of us over to his house down in his basement which was his trophy room. I had a broken collarbone at the time. I had my arm in a sling and he walked over and put his arm around me. We took a picture, so that was a pretty exciting time. He was a great guy and I was privileged to be able to play for him. It was well worth it.

"I've been told that the wishbone offense was made for your style of play"

Well it did suit a lot of my talents. My high school offense was basically a roll-out sprint out offense - making decisions on the corner as to whether to run the ball or pass the ball. I ran probably as much as I threw the ball in high school - easily 1000 yards rushing and 1000 yards passing in our games. I'd never been in a drop-back situation but in 69 and 70 that's all it was. It's not a comfortable situation for me, but I was able to hold on through spring training until he walked in and made the announcement that we were switching. I was maybe a little anxious but on the other side of that it was also encouraging because I knew that with an option offense I would have an opportunity to play. It's a beautiful offense based on the talent we had at the time. We had offensive lineman like Hannah, Kraph, Steve Sprayberry and some of those guys. They're going to move people out. The running backs like Johnny Musso, Rachelle Leah and Joe LaBue were a talented group of people. It just made sense to him, to put us in an offense that where we would be able to control the ball and control the game a great deal. With a passing game, 3 and out all the time puts a lot of pressure on your defense. I never saw the film of the Nebraska game after they had beat us so badly, but the other day I was surfing and I came across the Johnny Musso interview and there just happened to be a tag about the Nebraska game. I pulled it up and watched three quarters of it. It wasn't so pretty offensively but to see our defense the way they played that night was great. Terry Rowell was making plays all over the place and that's what the announcer kept saying. This guy is 5'11" and 177 pounds and he just kept making plays. Our whole defense - Robin Parkhouse, David McKinney. We just had a tremendous defense that kept us in good situations offensively. We never were in a lot of trouble when they were on the field they just took care of us. We tried to take care of them by not turning over the ball in bad situations.

"What was it like playing with Johnny Musso?"

It was great to have him on your side. He's a fantastic guy. Number one, he's just a great person, very humble but a terrific running back. If he had speed like they do today 4.6 or 4.5, there's no telling what Johnny would have done. He fell for as many yards as he ran because he would never just stop. He would struggle to get that extra yard. He was a terrific player and you knew if you needed a couple of yards you would get it with Johnny.

“What were some of the aspects of the wishbone offense that you remember?”

There was a certain terminology that Mal Moore used when we were learning the offense. It was “reach and flow” - reach back to the full-back and flow with him to the line. Go down and make a decision. We reached and flowed I don't know how many times but we did it over and over again. I remember when he made the announcement, he took the quarterbacks and we went down to the lower gym - just six quarterbacks and Coach Moore. We started working on the mechanics of the footwork and everything so you have to react quickly. It kind of falls into place. It wasn't that difficult and actually it turned out to fit pretty nicely.

“What about the secret practices and trying to keep it hush-hush?”

When I first got to Tuscaloosa they had curtains around the field, but they had never been used. I just kept wondering why we've got curtains here, but I found out that in situations, they put the curtains up around the practices when we went into that fall. Nobody could come close to it. Especially if they had any kind of situation where there were reporters around. I remember the night before we left to go to Southern Cal, he let the student body onto the field to cheer for us. He took the curtains down for that. Obviously we even disguised it for our own students. It was fun in that respect and also a little scary with a new offense. We were going out to play a very good team so there was a lot of anxiety.

"So let's talk about that first game with USC."

Yes, it was very exciting. The year before they had beat us so badly. I didn't know what to expect with a new offense. I knew we were going to be good at some point because we had a good offensive line. We had the running backs and the defense. Whether we had a quarterback or not was the question, so I was very nervous about it. It was the most anxious I've ever been for a football game - having to go out there and run this offense. I know there's some pictures that I've seen of our line firing off the ball on the snap and there's a gap. You don't even see the USC line, because our offensive line is just blowing them back off the line. We did a terrific job the first half controlling the football. The plays came in and everything worked just like we practiced it. I think we got a little conservative in the second half because we did not want to give up what we had and it turned out to be a pretty close game. They made some adjustments at halftime to try to take away some of the things that we were doing. To be able to go out and beat a team of that caliber under a new offense was fantastic.

"You might not have been the starting quarterback, right?"

There's no question about it. We had a guy named Billy Sexton, who was a great passer so had we not gone to the wishbone maybe I wouldn't have played. But it was just made for me. I guess being able to make decisions on the run which I did in high school - making decisions, reading the tackle and making pitches on the end. Those things just came pretty easy so it made the offense very smooth.

"What were of some of the aspects of playing the position?"

I can't say passing because we didn't throw the ball that much. We threw the ball as we went through the season a little bit more and then the second year we threw a good bit more. It's not an offense were you want to get behind, where you have to throw the ball. You've got receivers you can get to pretty quickly, so decision-making and being able to react to it without having to think was a big plus for me. I could react to what I saw pretty quickly. You had to run the read offense where you're checking the tackle to see if he's going up field. Cutting down on the fullback and what the defensive ends are doing. Sometimes both tackles are coming and the defensive end is coming, so you have got to be able to reach and flow and get rid of the football before that defensive end gets to you. I think it was well suited for what I had to offer.

"You were MVP both in 71 and 72 at the LSU game which one do you remember more?"

My junior year, I had a girlfriend that was at LSU, so that added a little more to it. Tiger Stadium was the loudest stadium I'd ever been in without a doubt. It was like trying to talk in a wind tunnel. I couldn't hear what I was saying. The huddle was like a scrum. Everybody was trying to hear what I was saying and I couldn't hear what I was saying. It was so distracting, from that standpoint that hurt me and maybe hurt the whole team a little bit in terms of execution. That noise factor was tremendous and they had a terrific football team. I was fortunate to ever win the game. I think Johnny got hurt during the game and didn't get to play much in the second half. The defense was what kept us in the game and kept us from losing. We were able to put up enough points to win, but it was a tough game. We had a very good team. The next year was in Birmingham with Bert Jones coming in, who was a terrific quarterback. Two undefeated teams playing each other. It was another big game and it just happened to be one of the best games I ever had in the two years offensively.

"Was there any play that stuck out in your mind?"

No, not really. We ran the basic offense. It was still early in maturity and the running offense wasn't quite where it should be. Anytime we had a defensive team that was tough, it put a little more pressure on us to execute a little better. The noise factor made it a little bit more difficult to hear as well if you wanted to make an audible at the line of scrimmage. So if you go against a team with the wishbone, defensively they're going to put 5 guys on one side and 6 on the other. You try to go where your strength is. It made it a little bit more difficult - not wanting to get into a bad play with the players not being able to hear. Other than that, the game gave us the most confidence.

"I heard about the LSU Tiger and the roar, I guess you remember that."

I remember hearing the roar, yeah it's quite a feature in Baton Rouge. I was there not too long ago, took my son out to the stadium and went over and saw the Tiger. I had to talk to him a little bit. LSU people are so passionate and fanatic about Tiger football. It's a great place to be on a Saturday night. Of course it's not so great if you're on the opposite side. It's a fun atmosphere.

"And what do you remember about the 1971 Iron Bowl"?

A lot of hype with Pat Sullivan and Auburn being undefeated and Pat winning the Heisman Trophy. Going against them, we were the underdog a little bit as far as quarterbacking goes. I guess that gives you a little more incentive to go out and try to play as well as you can. We did a couple things that they hadn't seen in terms of passing. We were able to throw the ball and loosen them up a little bit. The option plays worked great and Johnny had a great game running and the defense played well. They gave Pat one of the worst games he ever had. It was a tremendous game and all you could ask for in an Iron Bowl.

“What about the 1971 game against Tennessee?”

That was in Birmingham and they had a tremendous team - tremendous linebackers. Coach Bryant would generally let me call the plays and if they send in a play and you don't like it, they said you could run what you want. But you're not going to do that. If coach sends a play in, we're going to run it. We were not doing much in the first half. Somewhere during the third quarter they started sending in plays. We were just running from one side line to the other trying to outrun them. Their linebackers were just too good. I remember going off the field after one of those series and John David Crow was standing on the sidelines. He said, “Davis what's going on out there?” Before I could think I said, “if you'd let me call the plays!” He said you're exactly right. He went to coach Bryant and he never called another play. We went on to win the game about 32-15 I think. We were able to control them after that. It was a tough game. Tennessee was very good and they were an excellent defensive team.

“Do you think the wishbone is effective today?”

No I don't think so. When you look at what Georgia Tech is trying to do with it. When you've got men on defense today that can run for 4.4 and they are 6’7”. If you are tremendously strong offensively you can probably survive in your league because teams don't get a chance to practice against the wishbone that much. That was part of our advantage when we played because nobody in the league was running the wishbone. When you get out of your conference and go up against teams like Nebraska who were overall probably a better team than we were, it makes it tough. I don't know if you could live or die with just a pure Wishbone today.

"How about those tear away jerseys?"

What a neat event invention! Especially with somebody like Johnny Musso. I don't know how many jerseys you went through during the course of the year. It was probably is a little bit unfair. They finally outlawed the thing. Being a defensive guy and all you've got to hold on to at the end of the play is a piece of cloth you have a little bit of a disadvantage. But it was neat to have them and it was kind of a fun thing.

"What was your favorite football memory at Alabama?"

Well the 72 Tennessee game my senior year. They beat us up all day until the last two minutes of the game. We scored twice to win and it just so happens that I scored the winning touchdown. That was certainly a thrill and the LSU games overall. I think that being my home state and the school I wanted to go to, being able to win both those games was very exciting.

"Have you taken away anything about your relationships outside of college?"

Probably so. If you look at what Coach Bryant tried to teach us along with football. It was how to be better people. What are you going to do when there's not football? What kind of decisions are you going to be able to make? When I looked at the guys last night and know that they've all been successful and still look pretty good. It was due to the character that was built under Coach Bryant and all the coaches. He had a terrific coaching staff play for him who had learned his philosophy and what he stood for and what he expected from his players. All that went into providing us with a foundation that we would need beyond football, so it paid a lot of dividends outside of football.

“And what about Joe LaBue?”

Joe was always smiling. He's always happy and energetic. He never laid off on a play one time. He ran full speed all the time. It was a good boost to be around. I never saw him sad one day. He's always happy and a great guy.

The Tennessee game in Knoxville, my senior year in ’72, where they had us beat up all day until the last 2 ½ minutes of the game where we scored twice to win the game. As it happens I scored the winning touchdown.”

“Billy Sexton who was a terrific passer and had a great arm. I thought he was going to be my strongest competition. Had we not gone to the wishbone, maybe I would have played well eventually, but it was made for me, I guess

From 1970 to 1972 Terry threw for 1,328 yards and 14 touchdowns. He rushed for 865 yards and 16 touchdowns. He finished fifth in the 1972 Heisman voting and was the captain of the 1972 squad. Terry was the 1972 SEC Player of the Year.

Johnny Musso – Running Back – 1969-1971

"What was the atmosphere like in the program before the wishbone came along?"

You know Alabama had great success in the early to mid-sixties I don't know exactly what transpired but I think that the recruiting just fell off. We didn't have quite the talent that Alabama teams had in the past. My sophomore year during the '69 season was a very tough year as well as most every game that we played. During the '70 season coach Bryant hit the road and recruited hard. We had a lot of new talent but it was young. That '70 team really competed well and we could see at the end of that season that we were going to be a lot better team in '71. I'd say the atmosphere was hopeful. It had been discouraging the year before. People saw that we were making the turn and gave us a reason to have our hopes realized.

"Johnny what did you think about the change to the wishbone?"

That transition started my junior year. Alabama moving from a pass first option to a run first option. I had heard from my running back coach John David Crow. What a great privilege it was to be coached by him - a Heisman Trophy winner and all pro for many years. He was a great person and a great player. I got him the year that he retired from football, so he was very much a player's coach. He told me before we went to Houston in my junior year "gear up because we are going to run the ball. We're going to go to a hard-nosed, run first and do it by the basics the hard way". We ran the ball that game. It was a closely-contested game, but we won in a really solid performance. That started us to running the ball first like Namath, Sloan and Stabler. Run the ball first and run it second. It changed the last half of my senior year. When we went to practice in the spring of my senior year for the '71 season, we were going to be a tougher team. We were going to get back to the basics. We were going to run the football but we didn't expect the wishbone. It was a total surprise. Coach Bryant threw it out there that we were going to run the wishbone. It was all in and so I think it was a thing. We knew that we could run the ball and we were a tough team. Our line was really good. We had three All-Americans. John Hannah was All-American that year. The year following we had Buddy "bearcat" Brown and Jim Kraph so we had some great lineman and of course Billy Strickland, Jack White and Jimmy Rosser. We had some great all Americans that anchored that line. Going into that season Terry Davis was a great athlete. He could throw the ball on the run, but he wasn't a drop back. If we needed to make yards passing the ball, we just really didn't know what that would look like. It would be a different offense with Terry. We just really hadn't figured out how that was going to work. Going to the wishbone sure made sense. That was made for Terry Davis. I mean he never really got the recognition he deserved or earned. He was a great quarterback. I think he was the best wishbone quarterback or at least I don't think anybody did it better during the Alabama years but we didn't have anybody to compare him to because he was the first one. He made that offense go. He was the key to it.

"What were some of the skills that he had?"

One was just that he was really quick, not only mentally but he could make people miss. He really wanted to pitch the ball because he was sort of slight. He was tough but he wasn't physically imposing. He was always 5 or 10 yards downfield and he was always looking to give me the ball so as a running back it was always appreciated.

"How did you find out Coach Bryant was going to go to the wishbone?"

It was a surprise. He drew it up as, this is why we are going here. He talked about our strength as a team and he talked about how if we run this correctly we're going to have the defense outnumbered at the points of attack. He talked about the Texas staff coming down. They felt like they really knew the offense well and we could install it and perfect it. He said we're going to be a good team this year and we're going to be a good team with a drop-back offense. If we go to the wishbone and we do it right, we're going to be a great team. He laid the groundwork for us to be excited about it.

"Johnny why did you like it as a running back?"

I would much rather have run in a split back like we ran in the first two years but the wishbone that I ran in the final year was great. If I had run it three years, it might have become monotonous. You either went right and you were the lead blocker or you went left and you were the lead blocker. What you hoped was to get the pitch. Later they got more sophisticated with directing the ball where they wanted it to go. That first year was a true triple option, so you really didn't know if you were going to get the ball or not. So we had a few power plays. Basically for me as a running back I didn't know if I was going to run the ball. You either got the ball and went right or went left to block. It wasn't that complicated so I was glad that I got it that year for sure because we were a lot better team with it. Just as a running back it required a lot more of skills in variety of kinds of plays and different ways to attack from a split back.

"Johnny what do you remember about the reaction from the USC players when you lined up in that formation?"

I don't remember anything about it to tell you the truth. All I remember is when we got the ball the first few times we scored, because this team was so much better than we were. They had a lot more talent and they had beat us so bad the year before. It was hard to imagine how we going to muster whatever it took to beat them. We went down through that first drive and scored and I think that hope kind of turned into "hey we can do this". It turned into a firm conviction and the first three drives we scored 2 touchdowns and field goal. I don't recall that we scored much after that because they figured out what we were doing and they had a great team that year. They were preseason the first team in the country and they had beaten us pretty good the year before so we surprised them, but I also remember that all our scoring was done early.

"What was the significance of the 1971 season?"

The '71 season was a miracle. It was just a dream come true. It was just a magical year. The enthusiasm for the program had been a bit tough because we had performed just average the years before, but the fan base and the student's enthusiasm was just exciting. When you look back I think it was a page turning in Coach Bryant's career. It turned a new chapter in Alabama football. The 70s were his most productive years so it rejuvenated his enthusiasm. The wishbone was the perfect offense for him, but you had to play every play because if you got behind in the downs you had to make yards every down. It required a lot of mental toughness just to jam it down people's throats. So I think it turned a page in Alabama football, I really do. I think it was a banner year and kind of got Alabama back to doing things the hard way - the right way and I think you see that has reemerged these last few years in excitement.

"What about that injury?"

I had a dislocation, it just sort of popped out and was really inflamed so I missed the Miami game. It was the only game I missed in my career. For the Auburn game I had a bye week just before it, thank goodness, so I had about three weeks to get well but I was really very uncertain if I would be able to play. Coach Goostree knew how important that game was for me. He wanted me to be able to play so he came over to my room at night and gave me treatments and a lot during the day. I wouldn't have been able to play without his concerted effort. He made a plastic cast with moleskin inside of it, so I wore a 12 and a half shoe on my right foot and a nine and a half on my left. He was experimenting with that the last week, but before the game he had the final version of it. I went out and he gave me some hope that I was going to be able to play. It really did give me a lot of support although it was awkward with the bigger shoe. Coach Bryant wouldn't start me that game, but the other coaches talked him into letting me play and it started okay and as the game went on it got more comfortable.

I don't know that Alabama has ever been undefeated when they played a national game. It was amazing and exciting and I'm really glad that I had a chance to play and coach Goostree was really committed to making that happen.

"Johnny is that the most memorable game for you at Alabama?"

No, my sophomore year we had Ole Miss with Archie Manning, a night game at Legion Field and it was telecast on national TV so that was a great game. Now my junior year it was that Houston game because it was an unimportant game. One of the most gratifying wins I experienced were the USC and the Auburn games. I mean the first game I ever saw was Alabama and Auburn 1961. I snuck in the field with my cousins and older brother. We got there early and I got to see Coach Bryant get off the bus. Lee Roy Jordan was the man. I remember him walking off the bus and we watched Alabama get the national championship. It meant a lot to all the people in the state and it meant a lot to me. That's kind of where my dreams originated as a little kid. Watching that game and seeing the excitement and the majesty of it. So anytime we played Auburn it was an occasion. That last year playing an undefeated Auburn team for the national championship, it was really special.

“What do you remember about being recruited for Alabama?”

There were my heroes in Alabama like Lee Roy Jordan, Namath and snake, but when I looked at it Auburn was still emerging and they had a lot of enthusiasm and they had some good talent on their team. When it got down it to I just followed my heart. Coach Bryant came over to our house he sat down with my family and had dinner with us. I got a chance to talk to him one-on-one for an hour or two. I got to share my heart with him and what I really thought about my future. He just thought I would get every chance to fulfill whatever my dreams were. I really thought that I saw him as a person for the first time. I'll always remember that visit with him because that was real personal. You know I was a cocky senior and full of myself and I probably said some things I shouldn't have. I decided, I'll never say again and not in his presence. I think he got a sense of me and that I was hungry for things to do the things I wanted to do.

“Johnny what was your relationship with Coach Bryant?”

Some of the coaches told me that I was one of Coach Bryant's favorite players. I always knew that Coach Bryant liked me and he treated me well. He never said a bad thing about me. He knew what screws to turn or what tools to use to get people motivated. But to some people he was on them all the time because that's what motivated them best. But because I had that visit with him and he kind of heard my heart I think he knew that I was motivated. He just kept putting me out there in position and he let me start as a sophomore. He gave me a red jersey and I practiced with the first team. So that first practice didn't make any sense to me. I don't know that he's ever done that before but maybe he has. When I talked to him it was kind of like, you've got these things that you want to do and I'm going to give you the opportunity. From the first practice I practiced with the first-team offense and it didn't make any sense. I had to kill to stay there and he probably knew that. He treated me really well and he always talked well of me. I think he knew the flames that I had burning inside me. He was a great motivator. He knew what motivated me so I had a good relationship with him. But it was hard playing for Coach Bryant. It is not easy. All the teammates said they wouldn't give a million dollars if they hadn't had that privilege and opportunity, but they wouldn't do it again for all the money in the world. That's kind of true. It was a hard experience, but once you were done with it you realized the privilege of it.

"Johnny who gave you that name Italian Stallion?"

When it looked like I was going to start my sophomore year I remember after practice walking off the field and someone said, what's your nickname? I said Johnny well I don't have a nickname. He said no we have to give you one. In the course of several weeks he started throwing out nicknames and they were just awful. I said please don't go there and I totally forgot about it. When we played in Virginia our first game, I went to the pregame meeting. I was scared to death because I was going to play in my first game as a starter. I walked into the meeting and people were laughing and making horse noises. Then somebody showed me a paper and it said "Alabama to unleash the Italian Stallion". They had settled on that and that's the first time I heard it. At first I was kind of embarrassed by it to a degree, but people remember it. I guess my appreciation for that grew. I went to a lot of Italian-American father-son Banquets after my senior year in Pennsylvania and upstate New York and other places and still do.

"How did you end up playing in Canada with a fella named Carl Weathers? Do you think that had something to do with the movie Rocky?"

Well yes it had everything to do with that. Carl was a linebacker from San Diego State and he was a bodybuilder, so he was Cocky, Confident and outgoing. I'd come in the room and he'd say with a smirk, "Italian Stallion". He would always rib me about that. He was doing bit parts in the offseason and then he got that part as Apollo Creed. I never saw him again, but he's the common link. It kind of pissed me off that he used that. But the end of that story is Sports Illustrated did a 25 year "where are they now" piece and I was on the cover. They did an interview with me and asked me about the Italian Stallion. I was still kind of irritated because I hadn't heard from Carl. So I said his acting career started at linebacker and they wrote it just like that. I thought I got him a parting shot 25 years later, but I still never heard from him.

"To what extent has the wishbone extended to the offense in the present day?"

When coach was a player and they went to the Rose Bowl it established the foundation. So the wishbone established that foundation in the '71 season and onward. They created and built on that foundation and I think this was revived in the recent years. So I think we're that middle part of the tradition and left it in great shape for a new generation. Coach Saban shares a lot of the attributes of Coach Bryant. In his heart he wants to build young players into men of character.

The leadership ability he really wanted to see helped young men develop into men of character, good fathers and husbands. I think coach Saban carries that out very well. As a recruiter of people and he carries that out. I think that's where his heart is, so Alabama football is in good shape. It started with the people that made it something special for the next generation.

“What about the tear away jerseys?”

I don't know if it was 10 or 11 during that Auburn game. I think that it was in my junior year, the first time we wore tear away jerseys. We went through a lot of them and that was interesting. I started cutting them down at the waist. I only did it because I was losing so many jerseys and during the time out I had to change jerseys. I thought if it would be pinned at the bottom it would be less likely to tear. So I did that before one game and I liked it. The other backs noticed that I had cut that Jersey. I liked it a lot, when I cut it that second game Joe LaBue started cutting them shorter and Coach Bryant never said a word about it. So eventually Joe was cutting it shorter and shorter and finally he was cutting off half of the numbers. I said, “hey Joe leave my jerseys alone. I'll do it myself”. Everybody was cutting their jerseys off. In a short time that became kind of a trendy thing to do. It was fun. The first tear always were a lot of laundry, but it was a short-lived thing.

Johnny rushed for 2,741 yards and 34 touchdowns. He received for 495 yards and 4 touchdowns. He also passed for 2 touchdowns. He was #1 in the SEC for rushing yards in 1971 and 1972 and in 1971 for touchdowns. Johnny was an All-American in 1971 and inducted into the Alabama Sports Hall of Fame in 1989 and the College Football Hall of Fame in 2000.

Musso was a third round selection in the 1972 NFL draft by the Chicago Bears but chose an offer by the British Columbia Lions of the Canadian Football League. He played there from1972–1974, where he ran for 1029 yards in 1973 and was a West All-Star. He played for the Birmingham Vulcans of the WFL in 1975, rushing for 681 yards. After the WFL folded, he signed with the Bears in 1975 where he rushed for 365 yards and 6 touchdowns. He was selected to the Pro Bowl and First-Team All-Pro.

Joe LaBue – Running Back – 1970-1972

"How did you end up playing for Alabama?"

I was a boy who would dream when I was 11 years old in Birmingham growing up. That's when I start getting interested in learning about football and Coach Bryant. In 1961 they were the number one team in the nation. It started out as a little dream and it came to be.

"What's your favorite memory that you can share?"

Coach Donahue recruited in the Memphis area. He was the defensive line coach, so he would come up quite a bit. I went to high school in Memphis. I did have a few colleges that were recruiting me the day he came up. I had the official Alabama questionnaire with Crimson Tide on the top of it so it was a dream come true. That piece of paper was almost like magic to me. It meant so much.

"What do you remember about meeting Coach Bryant for the first time?"

He talked to us when we were freshmen in 1969. There was about 20 that went to summer school and we got there about the 1st of July. He talked to us and he told us a lot of things. He told us to make sure that we wrote home and tell your parents how much you love them. Tell them that you're going to be on a national championship team someday. There he was "the man". It's hard to explain the presence that he had. To have been there with him was a different feeling you had when you were around him. One of the things he told us was that I might give up on you, the assistant coaches might give up on you, your girlfriend might give up on you, even your parents might give up on you, but don't ever give up on yourself. Through the years, that's kind of stuck with me.

“What was the first time that Coach Bryant announced that they were going to the wishbone?”

We had kind of experimented with it a little bit. Coach Moore would take us in the gym with Terry, not the full team, and show us the mechanics of the quarterback position and the fullback position. Everybody knew about Texas running the wishbone and the great teams that they were having. So everybody kind of knew about them and they just dominated. He told us the first practice in 1971 that we were going to “sink or swim” with the wishbone - those were his words. We just had a job to do. There was no problem with us. We had been a passing team with Scott Hunter. The wishbone was just something that we all bought into. We didn't have time to ponder, because we had Southern California coming up. When we played that game we didn't have a lot of offensive plays. I think Terry Davis might have thrown two or three passes in that game. That was it and it was something that everyone just gave a great effort to and we had to get down to business.

“What do you remember about the secret practices?”

You hear a lot about the secret practices, but we were just taking care of business. I don't think we all got into the secrecy. Southern Cal had just demolished us the year before and we knew that we were going to face a football team that was just outstanding. They've always had a great tradition out there. As far as blocking, you had to be ready for the end doing certain things and the linebacker doing certain things. You really had to concentrate on those things and everything else just kind of took care of itself.

"What was your role in that victory?"

That game was a battle. They had some big guys. It was just a tough ball game and a great victory. I have never experienced such joy until after that game. It was a hard-fought game -17 to 10. There never was a game quite like that - Coach Bryant's 200th victory on his birthday in Los Angeles on a Friday night. We just totally surprised them with the wishbone. They had no idea. We even warmed up in the I formation that Thursday. Coach Bryant told us we're not going to run the wishbone in practice.

"Do you remember any specific plays in that game?"

The first couple plays of the game Musso was our fullback and of course he was our star player. Johnny was actually our left halfback, so Terry just handed off to Johnny. You could hear the Southern Cal players saying, "Musso's the fullback, Musso's the fullback!" That got their wheels spinning even more. After that Johnny just moved back to left half and Ellis Beck was our starting fullback at that time. We just marched down the field and I remember Johnny came back in the huddle in the second quarter. We had brand new McGregor helmets and it was a real light helmet. We were wearing white helmets that night and I looked at Johnny and his helmet was just busted wide open. I said, man you need another helmet, so he just jogged off the field.

"I heard you carried Coach Bryant off the field and he didn't normally like that did he?"

I don't think he minded it so much because nobody gave us much of a chance.

"What other games do you remember that the wishbone played a big part?"

The Auburn game that year. Pat Sullivan had just won the Heisman trophy. Evidently they interviewed Pat Sullivan and they asked him how do you think Alabama will do against Southern Cal? He made the comment. "I hope Alabama loses every game that they play" They put that up on the auditorium outside where we could see it every day so it was a truly great win.

"How about the LSU game?"

That was a battle and a half. Johnny Musso had gotten hurt early in the ball game so Wilbur Jackson came in and did a great job at left halfback. It was 14 to 7. Back then it was the only game on TV on Saturday night. When we were leaving the dressing room to go back out on the field they had that tiger and his head was about that big around. You had to walk around the cage to go out on the field and they had him right up to our door.

"Do you think the wishbone was the right style for that era?"

It suited us to a 'T'. When we started there in 1969, the program had sunk a little bit, but when we installed the wishbone it helped everything. It helped the defense get tougher. It was such a hard-hitting offense so the defense had to get tough. After we left the teams that followed us advanced it some.

“What's your favorite football memory?”

I would have to say the Southern Cal game. Here we are a bunch of smaller boys from Alabama on Hollywood Boulevard watching a movie. It was just a magical time. After the game, we went to Universal Studios. Those things just kind of surrounded the game itself. Just going out there and that long trip and the great trip back home. There was so many people in Birmingham waiting for us at the airport. There were thousands and thousands of people. I ran into my dad after the game and he said he had to park 2 miles from the airport.

Steve *Bisceglia – Fullback – 1971-1972*

At Alabama, Joe rushed for 928 yards and 5 touchdowns, and had 171 yards receiving for 1 touchdown. He was honored as #1 in the SEC for yards per attempt in 1971.

"What was your recruitment like at Alabama?"

I got recruited out of Junior College. A very dear member of the family played with Coach Bryant at Alabama and notified him that there was a player out in California that might be interested in Alabama. They had just graduated a fullback, Dave Bumgardner and they were looking for another pro-set running fullback to work with Johnny Musso. Johnny was going into his senior year and they were bringing in a coach, John David Crow, to give Johnny a shot at the Heisman, so they were looking for a fullback who knew how to run the pro set.

"What was it like playing the wishbone?"

It was a real thinking man's offense. The ball was snapped and we didn't know who was going to carry it so we had to be ready at all times.

"Terry Davis was the quarterback?"

Terry started and did a real good job with it. He was a magician. The full-back was the first option, so you always had to be ready to carry the ball. It was a different mindset than if you're blocking or faking or something like that. He would, in the first step, give me the ball and then if the defense had decided to take away the inside run, it was kind of a sad feeling because you were going to get hit from somewhere. He usually made the right decisions.

“What's so special about that offense?”

It's special in that you don't know who's going to carry it. As the defense unfolds, that's how the options are decided upon. It starts out looking like the same play every time, but it's not. When we went out to play USC, a little known fact is that we only had seven plays and a couple of pass patterns. We beat them and then came back and really got into it. I think the LSU game was when we really believed that we had something.

“In the Southern Cal game, what was the mindset of the players as they began to use the wishbone?”

It was interesting because I hadn't played the year before and now we were going out to play them. A couple of guys from my team from Fresno where I grew up were playing for USC at that time. I saw them during the summer and I was thinking we were going to run the pro set. It wasn't until I got back that fall that Coach Bryant announced the wishbone. Going out there we felt like we could play them this year. The year before we had a problem with them in Birmingham, but we had changed and Coach Bryant had changed. Everybody's feelings had changed and everybody was real positive about it so that was a big win for us.

“How had Coach Bryant changed?”

He had changed first of all by going from the passing game to the running game. Some coaching changes had been made that helped quite a bit. He brought in some new coaches and it was a year that change was in the wind - the whole situation with the blacks. I mean we had Wilbur Jackson and John Mitchell, the first blacks playing there and that was all part of it. That fit in and everything just came together. After the 71, 72 and 73 seasons and we won the National Championship, he started passing off of the wishbone. It really caused everybody fits. He made a decision that he was going to be moving ahead.

"What was it like having the first black players at that time?"

I wasn't that good of an athlete so I played as hard as I could on every play. I couldn't distinguish between black, white, green or purple. As far as in the dormitories and on the team you were judged by how hard you tried. That's what he judged it on - if Coach Bryant thought you were a good enough player and a man of character. Everybody on the team gave you the opportunity to prove yourself. He played the best 22 people he had. He played a lot of people. You knew you were going to get in the game, so you paid attention in practice - especially as the season built and we were getting more and more into the national picture. Maybe we would be playing for the national championship, but as far as the players it was based on your ability, work ethic and how hard you tried.

"What was it like getting ready and having the secret practices?"

I think one of the best things was that they didn't try to overload you too much. Terry came to the top quickly. I think Coach Moore worked with him a lot and had it down. Handling the offense and they kept it simple, even though there were a lot of options involved. A big part of it was getting Johnny Musso the ball. Getting it setup and getting the formations down so he would be in a position was important. Joe LaBue did a great job as far as blocking and Joe was a good ball carrier himself. Ellis Beck and I traded off half the time and there wasn't that much difference between the first and second string. I think that when I was there he was playing 54 guys a game. So you paid attention in practice because when you got out there with 80,000 people screaming and the clock running you would be ready.

"What were those practices like?"

As I remember them, they were intense. They were 90 minutes without the wind sprints afterwards. The segments and the periods were very well defined - what you were going to be doing. You would go live Tuesday and Wednesday, but you had to taper off because you were going to be playing on Saturday. The killer was in the spring. They could beat you up pretty good. There were a lot of skull sessions - what we're going to do. Such as implementing the game plan, first quarter game plan, 2nd quarter game plan.

"A lot of people have brought up LSU, Tennessee and Auburn. What do you remember about those games?"

I was unprepared for the intensity of the Southern Conference. Those games were just huge. Football in the west is entertainment, but football in the Southeast is serious. Tiger Stadium was really a great place to play. All week long Coach Bryant used to come up to me and put his arm around me and say, "Now Steve don't worry about that tiger. That thing is older than I am. Don't worry about that tiger, it's just a toothless hag." I didn't know that what they do is they roll out that tiger in front of your door, when you go out to play. When you go out, you're face to face with a

Bengal tiger growling at you. That got my attention, but we went out and had a tremendous game with them. Terry was from Louisiana, a home town boy coming back to play against them. So it was just a real hard-hitting game. The intensity of the games hasn't quit. They're just bigger, stronger and faster now, but the intensity is the same.

"How many times did you get the tear away jersey ripped off?"

When we played LSU I would go through 10 of them a game and Musso would go through 20. The rule was that your number had to show. If it didn't show, you had to go off the field and get it replaced. We had a system for that. Ellis would come in for the next guy and say "equipment change". At the 35-yard line would be the equipment manager holding up your jersey and you would turn tear off the old one and put on the new one. The running backs would go to the 50-yard line to get the play to come back in. Coach Bryant was always at the 50-yard line and Mal Moore as well. So we have this drive that we were doing and it was sputtering. Ellis came in and said equipment change and I looked at the 35-yard line and there was no one there. There was Coach Bryant holding my jersey and he said, "Come to me". I thought, oh no. When I got to him and he said, "What's going on out there, we're sending in these plays and they're audibling them out. We're sending in these plays for a reason. We're setting them up. Now tell them to run the plays that we send in there"! I changed my jersey and went back out and said in the huddle, run the plays that they send in. They said, what's the play? I said I don't know, just run the play! There were just moments like that that you remember. With this whole drive and series and the game going on, it was something really and other times you were focused so you had to stay with it.

"Is there another memory you can share about playing football at Alabama?"

There's lots of them. We had a game up in Tennessee. We were behind with a few minutes left, but we came back and beat them. I ran the ball down to the 2-yard line and in the next play Wilbur Jackson scored. We came off the field and everybody was surprised that we didn't go for two but the defense had them beat. So we came off and kicked and tied it. The defense held them and we got the ball back. In the huddle Terry looked at me and said, sorry. He called the same play that I had run before. About five guys hit me at the line of scrimmage and he went around the end for the touchdown to go ahead. There were little reminders like that.

"What do you think about the wishbone in today's game?"

I see a lot of variations of it. I think the game now is just so complex. When I look at the offense that Alabama's running now, you never see the same formation twice. It's just fascinating what they do as far as offense and I'm sure the defenses are just as complex. The teams that run the wishbone are difficult teams to stop, because most of the other teams don't use it. For the defense to try and figure out how to stop it is difficult. The team that's running it, I mean an Air Force or an Army, that's all they run. So they've seen every defense that you can throw at it. The big thing that Coach Bryant did was after our two years and throughout the rest of the 70s and into the 80s, he started passing. That was a game-changer. Now you've got the run option plus the pass option. That's a lot of what you see in these offenses. Some of these veers that they're running now - I think that's a big part of what the Auburn offense is now. But they'll figure out a way to man up on it. They have tremendous athletes now.

During 1971 and 1972 Steve rushed for 1,075 yards and scored 11 touchdowns. He also received for 1 touchdown.

Wilbur Jackson – Running Back – 1971-1973

"Why did you choose to attend Alabama?"

Easy choice - no other good offers. I got three other offers, but since Alabama had offered me the scholarship and recruited me I decided to go there.

"Were you recruited as a wide receiver?"

Yes and I played that position in my freshman year and then my sophomore year we went to the wishbone. I moved from wide receiver to running back.

"What was the conversation like when you made that move?"

He asked me if I had ever played any position in the backfield before in high school and I said yes. They said we're going to move you and some of the other receivers back to a position because we're going to go to the wishbone. I said okay I'll give it a try because I knew I could run and I was fast. How hard could it be? I didn't know until I tried it and it was a little bit harder than I thought it was going to be.

"What were the challenges?"

The biggest challenge was blocking - blocking on the corners. If you are running back for Coach Bryant in the wishbone offense and you couldn't block on the corners it didn't matter how good a runner you were - if you were willing to block on the corners for the others. Johnny Musso was the gold standard of the backfield. He was the toughest man in the field so we all looked up to him.

So my biggest challenge was not to just be able to run with the ball inside, which I hadn't done for a long time, but to learn how to block on the corners.

"What was your recollection about playing for John David Crow?"

He was a tough coach. Crow was a Heisman Trophy winner playing for Coach Bryant at Texas A&M. I think Coach Bryant made the statement that when he played it was like a man playing with boys and that's just how good he was.

"I think the first game when you had a headline was when you substituted for Johnny Musso"

After we had played LSU, I was getting a little bit of playing time. Johnny had gotten beaten up pretty badly and he wasn't going to be able to play. We didn't know that until later in that week. A long run on an option kind of relaxed me a lot – and one after that. The next week, Johnny made it back. That first game against Miami, that's one that I will always remember.

“Would you describe that touchdown run against Tennessee?”

Tennessee (1973) was one of our big rivalries. It wasn't a read, it was just a handoff. Everybody was going to the right and we had a first down already. Coach always preached about winning the game in the fourth quarter. He said we're going to be the best conditioned team. Class and pride will tell and we’ll win the game in the fourth quarter if it's close because we're better conditioned. We had scored in the very first play of the game and Tennessee had a great team that year also. By the fourth quarter of the game it was 21-21. That particular time, Coach Bryant went back to what his philosophy was. Because of the substitutions throughout the game, we should be in a lot of pressure. We scored three touchdowns in the 4th quarter - two were long runs and one was a big drive I just remember running and cutting back and a lot of guys picking up their blocks and 80 yards later there was a score. One play can make you or break you. If it was a fumble, it would have killed me, so that touchdown was probably my favorite.

“What was your relationship with Coach Bryant?”

He was just a good man, a hard worker. He was Nick Saban before Nick Saban - as a compliment for both of them. Coach Bryant was slightly ahead of his time. He knew that we had to go from the pro-style offense to the wishbone. We had a lot of good running backs, but he didn't think we had a good quarterback. He thought Terry Davis would be a good wishbone quarterback so his thinking was slightly ahead of his time in that sense. He would work you hard and he was very fair if you did what you were supposed to do. If he could help you out in any way that he could, he would. I can remember some games when we would come in at half-time and it would just be a tough game against Florida, LSU or Tennessee. They were never going to be runaway games. They were going to be tough, hard-nosed games right down to the 4th quarter. We would come in and it would be tight and instead of jumping on us he would say, we got a game today guys, we really got a game. That would loosen everybody up. But sometimes we would play somebody that we should be blowing out at halftime and it would be like 7-0 and it would be hard to be in the locker room. You couldn't wait to get out of there and get back on the field to redeem yourself, so I can't say enough about him.

In my sophomore year I was still playing wide receiver. In spring training I let a punt drop so we lost position there. I had dropped a couple of passes so he knew I was feeling bad. The spring game was never your last practice, there would be two or three after that, so he called me into his office. I remember him saying you never drop a pass because you want to - a quarterback never throws an interception because he wants to, so just relax and remain in control and everything's going to be better - but that punt you should have caught. I said yes sir and walked out the door.

The next moment I had with him was, nobody seemed to want to meet him head-on by themselves. One day in fall practice, you knew you had to wake up and go back out there. I remember we had a meeting, just the running backs and we were going down the hallway. Coach Bryant came out of his office and we were all going to meet him. There were eight or nine of us and one of him and he said, Wilbur, you're the leader of this crowd. You're the senior everybody's looking toward you. Whatever you do, that's what they're going to do. I wanted to say other things, but I said yes sir, I'll try to do better.

I remember Coach Bryant pulling me aside when I was a recruit and saying, I'll make you the best wide receiver in the nation. If you ever have any problems, you come and see me and we'll work it out. During the time I was there I never had to go and see him.

"What was the significance for you of being the first African-American to receive a scholarship from Alabama?"

The best part of that was to show how the team had evolved in the four years that I was there.

Here I came in and nobody else looked like me and 4 years later there were nine black guys on the team. Being elected co-captain - I was proud of the fact that I was judged by the kind of person that I was. I was proud of them as well and they realized that I was just the same as them. All we wanted to do was be in the games and have a good life for myself and my family.

"What can you share about Coach Mal Moore?"

Coach Moore for me was easy because he was not my position coach.

"How do you think the wishbone offense is in the game today?"

Today the game has changed so much. The wishbone was great in its time and everybody played the pro-style offense. At the time the wishbone was kind of a ground consuming offense so you could consume the clock. It was more like a tough man contest. Now you're running a hundred plays per game and you have to have the type of lineman to play the wishbone. Now you couldn't recruit that type of lineman to just be a straight blocker. Now everything has gone to the spread and now you have to have the right kind of quarterback to play the spread offense. The wishbone quarterback could probably not play the spread offense now and I don't think that the offensive lineman could play in the spread offense now.

Jackson wasfo the first black player to be offered a football scholarship at Alabama and was inducted into the Alabama Sports Hall of Fame in 2007. During 1971-1973 he rushed for 1,529 yards and 17 touchdowns. He was selected #1 for rushing yards per attempt by both the SEC and the NCAA in 1972 and 1973.

Wilbur was drafted in the first round of the 1974 NFL Draft by the 49ers. He played five seasons for San Francisco, and then three years with the Washington Redskins. In his 5 years at San Francisco he rushed for 2,955 yards and 10 touchdowns. He received for 1,233 yards and 3 touchdowns. In 3 years at Washington he rushed for 897 yards and 3 touchdowns and received for 339 yards and 1 touchdown.

Ellis Beck – Full Back – 1971-1973

"How did you end up playing for Alabama?"

I was recruited from Ozark, Alabama. I was in the 10th grade and I played on the varsity in 9th grade. A friend called ahead and they found out that I would have some potential as a college player. I had some good friends that started calling the University and I found out that they could take me to different football occasions. I attended several games in Birmingham and I attended a game in Mobile, when they played Southern Mississippi. When my head coach found out that I was being recruited by Alabama, he asked was there any other place that I would consider. Growing up in Florida, I said Florida State. My best friend's mother was a big Florida State fan. So I had my high school coach call Florida State. At that time they were going through some hard times athletically, so they said, oh come on down. Auburn was about 90 miles away so it was easy to drive up there on the weekend and spend some time with friends. I wanted to get a little further away from the house than 90 miles and I knew if I went to Tuscaloosa that my parents wouldn't be knocking on the door on the weekend.

"What do you remember most about meeting Coach Bryant for the first time?"

He had a mouth full of peanuts. He shook my hand and apologized for eating the peanuts and walked right off!

"What do you remember most about the installation of the wishbone offense?"

It was a shock. Scott Hunter had been the quarterback previously and they were using a pro set type offense. Unfortunately there was not a known passer to take Scott's place and Terry Davis was next in line. Terry was a good passer, but he was probably as good or better as a runner. He was so good at the option. It was just like he had natural talent for that versus being a long ball thrower. Quite honestly we had lost several good running backs and some great offensive lineman. The talent that remained just seemed such a great fit. I think Coach Bryant really took the talent that we had and used it. Back in those days you had curtains around the practice field and things like that, so it was not that difficult to keep it a secret until we showed up at Southern Cal.

"What do you remember about that Southern Cal game?"

I was named the starting fullback and we had a lot of good running backs so most of us didn't play 10 or 12 plays. You were out the whole game and somebody else took your place and they were as good as you were. Even though you might be starting off you weren't better than any of your other teammates. When we go out there to start Coach Bryant was afraid because I had never started any varsity game. I might jump off sides the first chance I got, so he didn't put me in the first play. He put Johnny Musso in my position and two other halfbacks in there and the next play they sent me in. They threw me a pass and everybody knew I had 10 thumbs, but I caught the thing and fell down. They had 90,000 people there and we were used to maybe 50,000 in Tuscaloosa so that was a pretty big deal.

"What do you remember most about Terry Davis?"

Terry was like a magician. He was the coolest guy I'd ever seen. Before we went to the wishbone Terry would walk into a huddle at practice and say, what do you want to run? He was so laid-back. You felt like you had as much input as he did in the huddle. When we changed and went to the wishbone, he was the chief. I remember we were playing LSU one time. He got to where he could option with either hand. One play he put the ball in his right hand and passed it off with his left. He just became so good at reading the defense and passing the ball. It was just meant for him to do.

"What about the Tennessee game?"

I always enjoyed playing Tennessee. All three years I played, we beat them. Tennessee was one of those teams that was coached a lot like Coach Bryant coached. When you were going to play Tennessee they were not the hardest-hitting, but they played collectively together so much better. If you were running the ball, you would get hit. It wouldn't be one or two hits, it would be three or four. But playing Mississippi State; they had some individuals that would just knock your head off. Tennessee just played together as a team and the only way that you could beat them is you had to play better as a team, but that's what the coaching was all about.

"How did the wishbone work so well winning the national title?"

We had the depth. We had Gary Rutledge and Richard Todd. Richard was a freshman and that was the second year they were letting freshman play. Gary Rutledge was in the line of Terry Davis. He was a very good passer, but he was just so good at controlling things and reading the defenses. The key to the wishbone was you either went to the right or you went to the left; it was very simple. As a fullback I had 5 Plays. I felt like I could play because I had run the wishbone in high school, so I was more familiar with it. It was so simple, if you had a good quarterback that read the defense, the defensive tackle specifically, you could run all day. You might get three yards or if they threw the ball maybe 30. It was a ground game of grind it down. You just ran down the field, but the quarterback was just so instrumental in choosing who gets the ball.

"What was the attitude like in Tuscaloosa when you won the National Championship in 73?"

I remember raising the window in the dorm and yelling when we were voted number one in 73. It was the third year in a row that we were in the number one position. Unfortunately we did get beat in the Sugar Bowl, however the polls at that time gave their number one position at the end of the season. I think there were four polls at that time, so we were able to secure the UPI national championship.

"What is your favorite memory about playing football at Alabama?"

People don't understand what you gain from Coach Bryant. It had more to do with life, than it ever did about football. In the summertime you would get a letter from Coach Bryant about some of his travels and they were always so personal. You knew that he was writing to a hundred and fifty people but it was always just like he was in the room talking to you. He would mention a few of the big stars that he had met, like Joe Namath but so much of the time the players that he mentioned were not the stars but someone who was good enough to be on scholarship, but might have played very little. They contributed more to your success than the stars did and that was so unique. When people ask me what did you learn most, I say a way of life. You learn so much from him because every day was different. He would tell you all the time what your life might be like after football. He would make up situations about your wife or your work. What are you going to do? Much of it was about life. He would just use football to try to make examples. I think that was the number one thing that I took away from Alabama. It became a way of life.

From 1971 to 1973 Ellis rushed for 1,129 yards and 6 touchdowns.

John Hannah – Offensive Line – 1970-1972

"What was your recruitment like at Alabama?"

There wasn't a whole lot of decisions to be made. I guess there were three schools that I was interested in but it was always Alabama because my dad and my uncle both had played there. My uncle had moved out to California and he was coaching at Cal State Fullerton. He started talking to me a little bit about going to Southern Cal and my mom was a professor at the University of Georgia. Those were the three schools that I was interested in. I came home and my dad said, have you decided yet? He said you can go anywhere you want. The one thing you have to worry about is, where are you going to eat when you come home? That kind of settled it. Dad was loyal. When dad was in the Navy, a friend talked him into going to college. Dad said where am I going to go to college? His friend said you're going to go to Clemson. So he went up there and said I got a half of a VA scholarship and if you can give me a half football scholarship and a bed to sleep in and three meals a day I'd like to try to play.

"What was your memory about the practice in 1971 when the wishbone was installed?"

We never knew about the wishbone on the offensive line. The quarterbacks had worked on it in a hidden way, but the rest of the team had no idea what was going on. We had to relearn everything. It was just a lot of work and rethinking on how you did things. We had to change our stance from a three to a four-point - just a lot of differences. For an offensive lineman, the wishbone offense is pretty easy. Basically one rule is that you come off and hit him in the mouth and that's about it. It was a good offense for offensive lineman because you were on the attack.

“What are your memories of traveling to Southern California to launch the wishbone in 1971?”

I remember we had received these new traveling uniforms, which were polyester. My pants were a little bit snug and when I went to sit down on the airplane I ripped the pants. That was all we had, so Mrs. Bryant gave me a blanket and sewed my pants up on the flight so I would have some clothes to wear when I got out to California. Strangely enough, the biggest memory I have of the game is how nice she was to do that. The game itself was really kind of a blur because it was just so intense. We felt we could win. We had determined in our mind that we were going to win. Luckily we surprised them and got ahead and held on. Of course that's the way Coach Bryant always did things - get ahead and hold on with defense the rest of the game. But it backfired on him a few times.

“How did you like the wishbone offense?”

I like it. It was good, but my favorite offense was the one I played with the New England Patriots. It fit me like a glove. It allowed the abilities that I had to shine. The wishbone limited big men. Everybody ridiculed the Patriots for drafting me because I was so small. Yet I was a big man at Alabama. Our coaches did not know how to coach big men. They kept trying to teach us techniques that were for smaller guys so that hurt a little bit. We weren't really able to use our abilities, but we quickly adapted. When Buddy Brown and the bigger guys came in, it was a learning experience for us and the coaches.

“It has been said that the key to the wishbone success was the offensive line”

I think it was the quarterbacks, not the offensive line. It takes a unique kind of guy and Terry Davis for us was that guy - very cool under pressure. We didn't have that predetermined kind of play. It was three options, so he ran it down the line and he would read that defensive guy. He handed off or he ran. The offensive line was very simple. I played guard, not tackle. Buddy Brown was the tackle. We would let that guy go and knock the defensive guy off the ball. It wasn't that hard and it wasn't that sophisticated. It was just smash mouth football.

"What was your experience playing with Terry Davis and Johnny Musso?"

Terry was made for the wishbone. He was an unbelievably cool, calm player. He had great peripheral vision. He could see behind him almost. I guess the best compliment I can make for Johnny Musso is that he made more yardage on one leg than most people made on two. You'd see him running and get hit. He would run on one leg for another five yards. He was just one of those guys that was all gut. He would never give up, so he was just a great ball player.

"What about Wilbur Jackson?"

Wilbur was an athlete. Wilbur was our first big running back at Alabama. He was about six one and probably weighed 190, so that was a big linebacker at Alabama in those days. Wilbur was fast, if he ever got outside he would fly. Because Wilbur was the first black athlete at Alabama it took a little time for him to get comfortable. After he did we hit it off, unfortunately it was during that time that racial issues still existed. Wilbur was not only a great athlete but a great gentleman.

"What would you like people to know about your experiences playing at Alabama?"

I enjoyed it. I enjoyed my teammates. The only regret I had was our last game against Auburn. Coach Bryant thought that offense was a necessary evil. If you think about it the wishbone is a defensive offense because you control the ball. Coach Bryant would say if you throw a pass there's only three things that can happen and two of them are bad. So he didn't like throwing the ball and he didn't like the option. I remember that Auburn game in 1972. We pounded it up the middle and they put 8 guys in the box. There's no way six guys can block eight guys, I don't care who you are. If he had let us open that offense up and really do what we can do, the punch would not have mattered. We screwed up on the punts so that's a thing that I'll have to live with the rest of my life.

"What about the 1972 Tennessee game?"

The defense made a big play and we got the ball back. I remember us having that gut check. That's when all of that stuff that Coach Bryant taught us came through for us. You know he always taught us that we could go further than we thought we could. I remember coming in the locker room and passing out those cigars. It was just a joyous occasion especially coming from behind like that. The wishbone offense is not a quick scoring type offense. It was just unbelievable the way those guys ran that ball the second and third effort and they finally got it in there. That might be one of the highlights the whole time I was at Alabama. It was something that really stood out.

John earned All-American honors twice. He was a Consensus All-American his senior year in 1972. He was named to the University of Alabama All-Century Team and also to the Alabama 1970s All-Decade team. He was inducted into the College Football Hall of Fame in 1999.

Hannah joined the Patriots in 1973. He excelled as a pass protector, a run blocker and as the pulling guard on sweeps. In the 1985 season Hannah helped guide the team to its first AFC title and Super Bowl appearance.

The Sporting News ranked him as the second greatest offensive lineman in NFL history. He was elected to the Pro Football Hall of Fame in 1991. Sports Illustrated featured him on its August 3, 1981, cover as, "The Best Offensive Lineman of All Time."

Jim Kraph – Offensive Line – 1970-1972

"What was going through the team's mind when Coach Bryant installed the wishbone?"

I was a middle linebacker at the time. The team had two things in mind. The defensive player could care less that offensive players were learning a whole new system. We did feel a little bit sorry for them.

"What was so effective about the wishbone in that era?"

I think the drive block made a huge difference because we were displacing the defense from the line of scrimmage by at least two yards on every play. It was a tremendous advantage to get a little space in there and let the quarterback operate.

"What do you remember about that time that the wishbone was installed in secrecy?"

I remember it was so secret that I didn't know they had changed it for a week. Coach Bryant came down from his tower one day and he asked me if I had ever played offensive line and I said no. He said I'm going to personally teach you how to block. It was probably the scariest thing in my life.

"What was the attitude of the team when you first played the University of Southern California and used the wishbone?"

We went out there and warmed up in the pro offense that we used to run. I think I even played with the defense, but I was moved to offense during the warm-up. Then we came out. Once the ball was snapped we just moved right down the field and everyone felt confident. We were level-headed, but we were very determined to get revenge.

Coach Bryant was such a unique person, obviously a brilliant football mind but I think he was a better human development person. He could just get people to play far beyond their capability. He could even have people fool themselves and think they were very good - as long as you were doing what he told you to do and you were very determined. Certainly anybody that played for Coach Bryant was physically very trim.

"What was your favorite memory playing football at Alabama?"

Just being with a great group of guys that were all out there fighting for the same because we really were a "band of brothers". We loved each other, that didn't mean that we wouldn't have a fist fight in the afternoon, but by the time we sat down to get something to eat that night we would share one piece of pie, so I think the oneness sticks out in my mind. I think Coach Bryant instilled that in us which made us work as a unit and it what takes a team to win a game.

After his career at Alabama, Jim played for the British Columbia Lions in the Canadian Football League.

Steve Sprayberry – Offensive Line – 1971-1973

"How did you end up at Alabama playing for Coach Bryant?"

There was no choice. But I have to go to school I was not a highly recruited player in their recruitment process. I wanted to go to Alabama. Mal Moore kidded me many times because Coach Bryant made the decision give me a chance.

"What made you want to go to Alabama so bad?"

I grew up an Alabama fan. I was 9 years old when Coach Bryant won his first national championship in 1961. One of the earliest things I remember about Coach Bryant was him talking on the television about his gutsy players. They weren't real big and not as talented as some others, but they had guts and something resonated about that. It never left me I just wanted to be a part of it.

"How awesome was that, after that memory to be part of a national championship team?"

It was a big thing. I came off of a state high school championship with a teammate from Alabama, Randy Billingsley and we both went to Alabama together. That was great. We grew from one championship up a level to another and that was very important. The process was an earned opportunity to go to Alabama but nothing was easy.

"What happened when he sat you down and said, we're going to go to the wishbone?"

Coach Bryant said, we're going to sink or swim with the wishbone so there was not any debate. He laid the gauntlet down so that was the plan. I was a sophomore trying to make that football team and you had seniors and this was their last chance to make that team so it was extremely hard. Jimmy Sharpe, our offensive line coach, made comments to some of the younger guys that were trying to make the team. I was trying to make that airplane ride out to Southern Cal and at least be a backup performer.

"How awesome was that when you actually got to go out there and win?"

It was tremendous. A good friend of mine said that when he was in graduate school in the early seventies they still talked about that in a public relations course. It was one of the greatest public relation ploys. They talk about that game in a totally different environment; not in athletics but in public relations how that came about. You couldn't do that today. There's no way. It was a fast very hard 4 weeks to get ready for Southern Cal.

"What is your memory about the secret practices over the three weeks you had to get ready?"

To me they weren't secret practices. It was the same thing that we would do otherwise. The offensive line did not change. The quarterbacks and the running backs and the formations they used changed, but the offensive line didn't. It didn't really affect us, but you understood about the process. You weren't talking about it and of course you did what Coach Bryant said.

"What other games do you remember where the wishbone really started to click?"

A very memorable game would be the Auburn game because Pat Sullivan had just won the Heisman trophy. They were a great football team but Alabama kept the football for about 38 minutes of the 60 minutes. It was a very big win for Alabama. There were close wins.

"Do you think the wishbone offense was the right scheme for that era?"

It was the right scheme for the players for sure. John Hannah was starting on offensive line the first year I started in 72. John could play any. He's probably the greatest offensive lineman that's ever been. He could win in any offense. The wishbone was perfect for me. We had the running backs to make it work. It's a very unselfish offense. The running backs blocked for each other. It's not like an offense where you've got a tailback who's not going to block anybody unless he's in pass protection. In the wishbone everybody blocked.

"Why was it so good for you?"

I wasn't the most talented player and we weren't as big as other players. I weighed about 225. Even as big as John Hannah was, he's not as large as those guys are today so for a smaller aggressive player that fit the bill for most of us.

"Do you think the wishbone could work in today's game?"

You still have some teams that will run it. Some of the military academies run versions of the wishbone so I can't say it couldn't work. But the rules have changed allowing you to use your hands on offense and the passing game has been enhanced. There's been a lot of changes that didn't exist back in the day. It's a very physical offense so the defense must be physical as well.

"Do you keep up with any of your teammates?"

Gary Rutledge is a guy that I see a lot. A lot of us keep in touch. We have had a reunion at our lake house for the last eight or nine years and we have a great turnout every year. It's a great opportunity for us to get together and talk and share. We've had coaches like Jimmy Sharpe come.

"What is your favorite memory about playing for Alabama?"

The great wins of course. We had some games that we won with a lot of points and we had some that we had to really come from behind. Against Tennessee in 1972 my junior year, we scored 2 touchdowns in like 2 minutes to win that ball game. I'll never forget that it was tremendous win. In 1973 when we got behind after beating California 66 to nothing in the first game of the season. We got behind 14 to nothing with Kentucky. Coach Bryant said in the locker room, I'm glad we're in this position right now so we're going to find out how special you guys really are. In the second half after the kickoff we ran for a touchdown and we won that game 28 to 14. We got into another tough situation with Georgia and had to score two touchdowns in the last few minutes of the game. Those kinds of things are Alabama football. We were trained to react to situations like that. Coach Bryant and the other coaches trained us pretty hard to handle situations like that. That's the kind of thing that you really remember.

Wayne Wheeler – Wide Receiver – 1971-1973

"How did you end up at Alabama playing for Coach Bryant?"

I'm from Florida, so Florida started recruiting me as a 10th grader. I thought I was going to Florida and never heard a word from Alabama. One of my friends went to Alabama the year before and he ended up an All-American defensive end. Alabama finally called and said we're going to offer you a scholarship and as soon as they did I said I'll take it. My parents were not real happy about that because they wanted me to go to Florida. The Alabama coaches called us in a room and said you're going to hate it here, but if you want to be a national champion this is the place to be. There weren't very many guys from Florida up there but it ended up being good for us.

"So what was it like being from Florida and coming up to Tuscaloosa?"

They said it was going to be tough. We were brought up a little bit more liberally so we didn't have the rules that they had when we came to Alabama - even hair rules. You had to have your sideburns cut above your ears and short hair. That was in the seventies and everybody was sort of a hippie. We stuck out and we didn't like it then, but I can see now it was a matter of everyone being the same and it worked.

"What do you remember about the installing of the wishbone offense?"

I was a receiver and at that time they were playing a pro set and we had a lot of receivers. You had to, but when you go to the wishbone you only had one receiver and you didn't throw to him very much. It ended up being a good thing for me as I did have speed. In the wishbone when you're running a ball that defensive back only has to take one step. If you're fast enough, you are by him. I think I had 27 yards per catch and that's just because everything that we threw was a bomb, it was make it or not.

It didn't start out that way. Really we were blockers for the backs. Every play you went down field and you tried to drive your corner back and then stop and block because if he broke through the line that was the last man that could have stopped him. Fortunately as the wishbone progressed they did start throwing the ball a little bit. Now you can stand down field and they would take one step up try to stop the run. You're gone. All the quarterback has to do is put it somewhere in the vicinity and they'll find it.

"Take me through that famous play in the Tennessee game"

People always talk about that play and Coach Sharpe likes to tell us the whole story about how that developed. It was a lot different than what I thought it was. I thought they were setting that play up. They always ran a dive first play of the game and I was thinking, I wish we would throw one time on 1st down or do something different. When they told me they were thinking about doing that against Tennessee I thought that they had set that up. In other words they were intentionally running a dive every play with the intention of using it against a team they really wanted to surprise to find out what their intentions were. We realized we're always running the ball every time. Let's try something different. Coach Moore went to Coach Bryant and said, let's try to throw the ball on first play. They said he put it on the board and Coach Bryant kind of digested it for a whole week and let them know on game day that they were going to try it. I was surprised that they did it because we were so deep in our own end zone. I think we were on the 20-yard line and that isn't it generally where you throw a bomb, but it worked great. 80 yards and I had to start laughing when I went by the guy because he didn't know.

“Was there another play or game that sticks out in your mind?”

I always enjoyed playing LSU. We always threw a lot of passes against LSU. I found out that Johnny Musso’s foot hurt. Then I started, that's why we threw because some of the better guys were hurt.

“What was it like playing with those guys?”

It was great. The team unity was just amazing. I think that's why I went to Alabama instead of Florida. I think our goals were all the same. Some people had better luck than others. Overall it was a team effort. We didn't have a superstar. There were some players that stood out, but we didn't necessarily count on them. We played as a team - every guy had to do his job.

“What is your opinion about Gary Rutledge as a wishbone quarterback?”

He was fine with me. He got my name in the books with that pass. I'm thankful to be remembered for anything.

“How do you compare him to Terry Davis?”

I had a much better year my junior year then my senior year. I don't know if it was because we were a better team at running the ball as a senior but they threw the ball a lot more my junior year. I think I only had about three touchdowns my senior year and I had maybe 11 in my junior year. So from that respect Coach Bryant for whatever reason seemed to give Terry a lot of leeway to throw the ball that he didn't seem to give Gary Rutledge at that time. We were pretty strong runners. I'm somewhat amazed because I'm not from Alabama. I'm amazed that some of these people remember stuff that happened 40 years ago. I've never been that way. I do something and then forget about it. I do appreciate it. The players from Florida did interesting, amazing things but you don't hear about that anymore. If you have one good play at Alabama you're remembered forever.

"What is your favorite memory that sticks out in your mind?"

I was married three days before I went up to Alabama and I knew that you didn't tell them that you were married because they would pull out your scholarship. I didn't tell anyone. Every once in a while they would reward freshman for doing something a little bit above average in practice. They would let you go in and eat at the training table. I got to do that one night. Most of the other guys had left and Coach Bryant walked through the door and he sat down next to me. Coach Bryant didn't do a lot of talking; he did a lot of listening. Because I wasn't going to the game, Coach Bryant asked, what are you doing this weekend. I very innocently said, I'm going home to see my wife in Orlando. He started coughing and he looked at me and he said, you are married? I said, yes sir, I got married 3 days before I came up. After that we started having a lot of married players. I think he realized he didn't have to supervise us. Living in a dorm guys would go a little bit crazy. Well I had a wife at home that I had to report to so he finally started changing his philosophy. We ended up with a lot of guys married on the team by the time I graduated but it was a scary thing when I slipped.

At Alabama, Wayne rushed for 1,246 yards and scored 11 touchdowns. He was #1 in the SEC in 1972 for receiving yards. He played 12 games for the Chicago Bears in 1974.

The Rutledge Brothers

Gary and Jeff Rutledge both played quarterback at Alabama for Coach Bryant in the wishbone era. Both wore the number **11** jersey. Each had a national championship – Gary in 1973 and Jeff in 1978. Gary was the MVP of the SEC in 1973. Jeff was MVP in the 35-6 victory over Ohio State in 1978 Sugar Bowl.

Gary Rutledge – Quarterback – 1971-1974

How were you recruited for Alabama?"

Well I wasn't a highly sought-after quarterback out of high school. Coach Gryska was the one who recruited me. I was not even recruited by Coach Bryant but he knew about me. I met him when I came on campus. The main thing is, I always wanted to go to Alabama. My dad took me and Jeff to football games all the time. I remember watching Kenny Stabler run against Auburn for that touchdown. I went to many games and always as a kid I wanted to play for Coach Bryant and Alabama, but how many people get to do that? I was blessed.

"What was it like when you finally got there?"

It was hard to believe. It really was. I couldn't believe I was going to Alabama. I really didn't think about it until I got there, but the year before I came to Alabama they signed about six or seven quarterbacks. But that didn't bother me. I just wanted to go to Alabama and play for Coach Bryant. In my mind I didn't know whether I would play or not, but to come here and compete and try to play was great. Luckily I got to play.

"What do you remember about playing the wishbone?"

Well I was redshirted that year. I was a true sophomore. That summer we came in to a team meeting and they said we're changing offenses. We haven't been successful in what we've been running so we're going to the wishbone. Do not tell your closest friends, your parents, your brother and sister or anybody. Even that fall when they had the sports writers come to town, they had us run the old offense from the previous year. That was a real surprise thing going against Southern California. I really didn't play that year. Again I was redshirted which means I was the other team's quarterback in practice. All that year I was getting pounded on by that defense.

“Was it hard to keep it a secret?”

Not really, I enjoyed the fact that nobody knew. I just wanted to see what was going to happen. The whole state of Alabama, like it is today, follows Alabama football. Even though I wasn't going to be a part of it, I watched it on TV in Birmingham.

“Take me back to that game against Tennessee”

Well the first play of the game, we planned it all week. I think that was the fifth or sixth game of the year. The first play of the game, we ran the offense to the fullback because we wanted to see who was going to cover the fullback, who was going to cover the quarterback and who is going to cover the pitch. We wanted to know their defensive plan and their scheme against our wishbone. We had watched Tennessee the previous week so we just turned and faked to the fullback and I left the ball on my hip. Wayne was wide open. I mean it was a scary pass. People might look at it and say he was wide open. To miss a pass either short or too long would have been hard on my career. It was planned and it worked successfully.

“After the 1973 LSU game you were featured on the cover of Sports Illustrated with Coach Bryant. What do you remember about that?”

Well, if I had my best game ever, that was it. It was 21 to 7 and I threw two touchdowns and ran one. Never in my wildest dreams did I think I would do something like that. The team was so good in that game. We dominated LSU. People don't talk about the '73 defense, but we had a great game. Our offense was unstoppable. People hadn't figured out how to defend against the wishbone and we just ran our offense to perfection. That night it was fun to see the LSU fans quiet up by little bit. I remember walking around the field before the game and they were throwing oranges at us and they were splattering everywhere, so it was a neat experience to go through.

"What was your relationship like with Coach Bryant?"

Coach Bryant was a different kind of head coach and I really didn't have a relationship with him. I had a better relationship than most folks on the team. As quarterbacks, we would take a walk before the game, the pre-game meal. We would take a walk with him and Mal Moore. This was always a time where he could tell us to show class, run the ball behind your best blocker - just the little things like that every week. Coach Moore would talk about the game plan, what to do in certain situations like third-and-short, third-and-long or whatever. He would touch on that, but like many people I really didn't have a close relationship with Coach Bryant.

"What about your relationship with your brother, wearing the same number?"

It was really neat. We have set an NCAA record that people don't know about. We're the only two brother quarterbacks that have started in all 11 games for a national championship team. Jeff and I had always been close growing up. I remember my senior year and Jeff's senior year of high school. He could throw the ball further and better than I could. I was starting at Alabama, so I couldn't figure that one out. I tried to get him to Alabama at the time and I worked with him a little bit that summer before he came to Alabama, learning how to do the wishbone. Today we have a good time signing autographs, but I can't believe people would want my autograph. I was blessed to play here at Alabama for Coach Bryant.

"Is there anything that stands out with your time at Alabama?"

There's this story I can tell about Coach Bryant. My dad chewed out Coach Bryant! The year we went to the wishbone, I was redshirted. We always had to take buses to get down to the stadium, so my dad came down to watch the scrimmage. We were in the wishbone again and I didn't get into play in that scrimmage. Well, my dad was very upset because he knew I could run the wishbone. I had run a veer offense in high school where you do a run and read. After the scrimmage we were all piling on the bus to go back to the coliseum and I looked out the window. There's my dad nose-to-nose with Coach Bryant chewing him out! You can imagine what I thought. Here's a legend being chewed out by my scrawny daddy, saying let my son play! I'll never forget the dread that I felt. My dad always said if he hadn't chewed out Coach Bryant, you wouldn't have played. After that when Coach Bryant would see dad at a game, he would go up to my dad and say, "Mr. Rutledge you aren't going to hit me today are you?" So it was a neat story.

"Were you aware at the time that you were going to be part of Alabama football history with the wishbone?"

No, never in my wildest dreams did I think that I was going to be part of history with the wishbone. I wished many times that at the time I had kept a diary of all the practices, players and things that we went through - the experiences and emotions in 1973. As I look at it now especially with the wishbone, and the games we won, it's just an honor to be part of that.

"So how would you describe the position that the wishbone has had in Alabama football?"

Back in those days it was before ESPN. I think there were only one or two games a weekend. Although we were on four times, maybe five in 1973, the importance in those days was not as great as it is now. It makes me feel good and I'm just honored to be a part of this.

"How competitive are you with your brother?"

In football we weren't, but ping pong, pool, golf and tennis - yeah we were competitive. I was always proud of Jeff. He had more ability than I did and I kid people that I'm Jeff's brother!

"How important was it for Coach Bryant to switch to the wishbone offense?"

It was very important. He would tell you in books that you read that in the previous years he thought he had a really good team and a really good offense, but he wasn't winning. He couldn't understand why. Coach Bryant was smart enough and innovative enough and not afraid to ask other coaches, what can I do to be successful because I know that I've got the players. I've got to get something else going here. So he asked Darrell Royal and the folks out there about the wishbone. He sent his staff out there. He wasn't afraid to change. You have to admire Coach Bryant, when you look at the seventies and the winning percentage. It was the smartest move any coach could have made.

"Did you have a Playbook?"

No, there wasn't any playbook that I remember. We didn't have that many plays when we first started. When we went to Southern Cal we only had about six or eight plays so it was a simple offense. When you get the ball from the center, you don't know which of the three options you will use - who's going to take the ball because you're reading the defense as soon as the ball is snapped. If that tackle takes the fullback, that's the first option, so it's either pitch or keep. If I keep it, that's option 2, if I pitch it that's option 3. If you read the defense properly, there's no way to stop it.

"How would you describe the legacy of the wishbone in Alabama football history?"

It's got to be up there. Coach Saban is building his own history, but Coach Bryant had his legacy. Coach Bryant had Joe Namath and Kenny Stabler of course. But you have to think of the '70s. I mean how many teams can win 3 national championships with the wishbone offense within a 10-year span? His legacy here was built on the wishbone and it was a pretty neat thing to be a part of.

Gary passed for 1,119 yards 43 times yielding 11 touchdowns. He also rushed for 10 touchdowns.

Jeff Rutledge – Quarterback – 1975-1978

"How were you recruited by Alabama?"

I was very fortunate to be recruited by a lot of schools. Alabama had gone to the wishbone obviously with my brother. I was really a better passer and I felt like I was a good runner in high school. I was running the veer. I considered going to other schools because I didn't want to run the wishbone. They weren't throwing the ball very much then. My choices got down to Alabama and LSU, but I always was an Alabama fan and I went to games with my dad and my brother. However, I wanted to throw the football and when they went to the wishbone they didn't throw it as much.

"What were some of your favorite plays?'

The audible. In the wishbone you would get what I called "zero coverage" and I had Ozzie Newsome, one of the best to ever play, out there at wide receiver one on one. So Coach Moore would give us the permission to check off. I can't remember how we called the audible but our post was "check 8, check 8", ride the wishbone, come back and throw the post. Ozzie would be wide open and it gave you a lot of choices in the wishbone to throw the football. In certain situations, Coach Moore would give us the option to do it, but the wishbone was about running the football. That's what we did. Now teams are doing that and that's what you've got to be able to do - run the football and that's what we did.

"What do you remember about the Sugar Bowl against Ohio State?"

I remember I was getting married the Saturday after the game. We had a chance during that game to win the national championship. We were ranked four or five and Notre Dame was behind us against Texas. It was a great game and we beat them 35-7. I was fortunate enough to get MVP for that game thinking we were going to win the national championship but we ended up number two in the polls. I remember that it couldn't have gone any better. We were throwing the ball and running the ball. The best picture I have of Coach Bryant and myself was at the press conference with NBC and I'm looking up at Coach Bryant and he is saying "nice wedding present son".

"What do you remember about the 1977 USC?"

I remember coming out of that game thinking that I took a lot of shots. When you run the wishbone the defense always felt that the quarterback was going to run the ball. Even if you read the wishbone, the defense couldn't tell a lot of times who had the ball so I would get hit. I was thinking I got a late hit, but even the officials couldn't see who had the ball so I remember coming out of that game being really beat up.

"What about the 1979 Sugar Bowl?"

I just remember it was a defensive battle and of course I remember the famous goal line stand. The play that I think a lot of people don't talk about was when Don McNeil knocked the running back out. That guy was going right into the end zone to score and they ran like three plays up the middle and our defense stopped them. A great feeling obviously to see that when you're in that situation.

In the Pitch to Major Ogilvie, you're going to get hit. Obviously in a triple option you're going to get hit. You end up on the ground half the time and a lot of times you didn't see the run but when you ran it right it was really tough to stop.

“What was your relationship with Coach Bryant?”

I think it was a great relationship. Coach Moore was my quarterback coach and all our meetings were done in his office. Coach Bryant would come by and say his opinion on what we were talking about. It was a great relationship. You knew that he cared about you and you did nothing but want to please him.

“And Coach Bryant would talk with his quarterback?”

When I came to Alabama, my brother had told me just about everything to expect. What was funny was coach would give the same speech every week. It was, when to pass and when not to pass when the defense least expects it. That's pretty much common sense and it was the same week in and week out. But the thing that I remember still to this day was at the end he would turn and say, “Be brave, be brave” and he said that every week. It was an honor to play for him.

“And your brother prepared you, he told you what to expect?”

Gary and I were very close and I knew what to expect when I came here. I felt he didn't get the credit that he deserved, but he wasn't recruited very heavily. He came here, he did nothing but earn his way in. I knew how hard it was for him and how he fought to win the starting job. It was great to see him win the national championship. When I came down here, I felt like I was following in his footsteps. A lot of brothers don't want to wear the same numbers, but I wanted to because he had that much of an impact on me. We were very close then and we're very close now. We would play ball together and played against each other, but I was his biggest fan and he was my biggest fan. It was an honor to come down here and take his number. A lot of guys didn't want to be in their brother's number but I wanted to.

"The 1973 season starter, what do you remember about that game?"

I was sitting in the other end zone and I told the people sitting around me what the first play of the game was going to be. Gary is going to fake it to the fullback and pass down the field. They ran it for a touchdown and these people were looking at me. How did you know that? I can't believe you knew that? I did not tell them the whole game who I was, but Gary had told me!

"Were you aware that you were going to be a very special part of Alabama's football history?"

I don't know if it really sank in. I was just a part of Alabama football and it was enough for me to be able to come and follow in the footsteps of a lot of quarterbacks. Just to be able to follow my brother and Richard Todd and to be able to just play for Alabama and the wishbone. I think at the time I threw it more than any other any other wishbone quarterback. I remember asking Coach Bryant, if I come to Alabama, am I going to throw the football more? He looked at me and said, "Not if I don't have to". That's really not what I wanted to hear, but it was so true. You look at teams today and they throw about 25 or 30 times a game to win a National Championship. Even Alabama's throwing the ball 25 or 30 times a game. I had reached maybe 7 times a game and we won the national championship. You didn't come to Alabama to throw the ball, you came to Alabama to win national championships and that's what the wishbone did.

“How special was it that you shared that bond with your brother?”

Well it's special. I didn't realize this until a few years ago. Somebody did a story that we were the only two brothers that have won a national championship while playing quarterback. That was special. The relationship that my brother and I have make it special.

“What was it like to follow in his footsteps?”

It was an honor and I wanted to follow him and wear his number 11.

“Why was the wishbone so special and what made it work?”

It starts with the guys up front. It was dropped on everyone for the USC game. The guys up front would make the holes, and then you had to run it with perfection. There was so much pressure to read it right. Everything was pretty much a read. There were very few plays that you called in the huddle that you did exactly what was called. You had to read the tackle. You had to read the end and you would either run it or pitch it. It was not very often that you would throw the ball because you would get one on one coverage. A lot of reading was going on in the passing game so the wishbone was execution. If you didn't work it well, you weren't going to get the results. In practice it was a pretty much live situation. You had to run at full speed in practice or you weren't going to get a good picture of what was going to happen.

“So what is the impact of the wishbone on today's game?”

When you think football, you think toughness. I mean you've got to be tough. In the wishbone you had to have the guys up there in front that were tough - that could control the line of scrimmage. They came out low and they didn't stand up. The way you think about football is, the toughest guys are going to win and we had nothing but tough guys. Coach Bryant would dress 75 players and play 75 players and that is the way we practiced and that is the way we played. I think the wishbone would wear people out. We would just keep getting new people in the ball game and no one can argue with the success that we had with that.

While at Alabama, Jeff completed 207 passes for 3,351 yards and 30 touchdowns. He rushed for 546 yards and 11 touchdowns.

Drafted in the1979 NFL Draft by the Los Angeles Rams, Rutledge played in 14 NFL seasons from 1979 to 1992 for three different teams the Rams, Giants and Redskins. As a member of the Redskins, he came off the bench in a game versus the Detroit Lions in 1990. Trailing 35-14 with 10:37 left in the third quarter Rutledge led a great comeback. He completed 30 of 42 passes for 363 yards and a touchdown and rushed for 12 yards for the game-tying touchdown with only 24 seconds remaining.

He was quarterback's coach for Vanderbilt from 1995 – 2001.In 2007 Rutledge got his first NFL coaching job when he was hired as quarterback's coach with the Arizona Cardinals.

Richard Todd – Quarterback – 1973-1975

"How about your recruitment to Alabama"

Recruitment to Alabama was really unusual back in 1971. That's when Auburn had Pat Sullivan. So I actually committed to Auburn, but the bottom line was that I wanted to play for Coach Bryant. So before I signed I had a lot of influence on me because my dad got his Doctorate from Alabama. I didn't go to Alabama because of the wishbone. We used an option offense in high school. I liked to throw the ball and we threw it quite a bit.

"What do you think about the wishbone offense?"

It took a little while for me to get used to it, but what a team offense it was. We had great running backs. We had Wilbur Jackson and Shelby. Wilbur Jackson still has the record for yards scored per attempt. The way that Coach Bryant did it was, if it's in the first quarter, he would put in the first team offense. I was the backup. If it's 0 to 0, we're up 14 to 0 or were down 14 to 0, Coach Bryant would say give me the second team backs and the third team line. So we just switched players in and out. I learned to like it. We just wore people down. We had a great defense. We had a bunch of all Americans on defense, but we never did on offense because we played so many people. We would play two or three quarterbacks a game and three or four running backs. But everybody wanted to play more.

"What do you recall about the tear away jerseys?"

I've got some great pictures of tear away jerseys. You know you'd be running through your line and they would tear away. I mean you just touched a finger on them and they would just rip. We kept coming off the field to change our jersey. All the running backs and quarterbacks would do this.

“How did you like playing with the wide receivers?”

I loved playing with them, but I just wish we had thrown more. I think that in my senior year we were throwing the ball six times per game. We really didn't need to throw the ball that much.

“What are your memories about playing Penn State in the Sugar Bowl?”

That was a crazy time in Alabama because I think we had lost six or seven ball games in a row. Penn State had a great team. What I remember was that it was just a grind out game. It was a real hard fought game. I remember Joe Paterno coming in our locker room and shaking everybody's hand. He came up to me and said, “I didn't think you could throw the ball”. I think I was 10 for 12 in that game.

“How would you compare the wishbone offense to the option offenses of today?”

I played in the pro offense for 11 years. Today you get more people in space. They don't rely on the running backs the way that they did back in my day. You find the weak point and you've got 4 or 5 wide receivers out there. If you've got a running quarterback, you can run the option. It depends on the personnel.

"How do you feel about the championship team in 1973?"

Well we did get beat by Notre Dame, so we were the UPI national champions and they were the AP. I think that we had the best team in the country that year by far. That game was a great ball game. We had so many great players.

"What was your relationship with Coach Bryant?"

I tried to stay away from Coach Bryant. I stuttered a lot, so he probably didn't want to be around me either. Coach Bryant is a lot like Saban. He expects the best. You have to do your job and not worry about the things around you like the noise. Just concentrate on what you're doing. It was a lot of fun.

"What are some of your special memories playing at Alabama?"

ru

Playing for Coach Bryant didn't really hit me until after I was done playing pro ball. When you're in college and playing football and see him every day you didn't really think about it. Now looking back at everything he has done, it's just a privilege and a pleasure to play for somebody like that.

"Do you have any special memories about your teammates?"

I've got a lot of good friends and I still keep in touch with them. It would have to be the Auburn game. We beat them every year - my sophomore, junior and senior year. The Penn State game when we broke the bowl streak was special. They were just my buddies. We had so many great athletes, it's just incredible. I can't name them all.

"Any other interesting stories you would like to share?"

Mal Moore was my quarterback coach. He ended up being a really good friend of mine and we kept in touch. All the time he would grab my face mask. I was a sophomore starting out and he would just rip me to the ground and you get kind of tired of that. He did it all the time, so I started spitting on this face mask. Sure enough after about 5 minutes in this drill he comes up and grabs my face mask. He never grabbed it again.

The other story would be in the Sugar Bowl. That was in my senior year. Coach Bryant was going to do something different. We had lost five or six games in a row. We would always go down to the games on a Saturday and then on Thursday and Friday we would practice and then play the game. We all went down to New Orleans a week before the game and that was a big deal to us. There was no curfew the first night, Monday or Tuesday. There was a curfew on Wednesday so we thought we've got one more night. There were about 22 of us I think there were 11 starters. We stayed out late and you heard the scuttlebutt the next morning. At breakfast Coach Bryant stood up and read off everybody's name that had broken the curfew. I can't repeat all the words that he used, but he looked at me and, "Richard Todd, our newly elected Captain came in at 2:30!" I'm going to take everybody's name and send it to your hometown paper. You were out late, so if we lose this ball game they won't blame me. Sure enough he did that, so thank goodness we won. Years after that Mal and I would talk about it. He said that morning when Coach Bryant came in and found out, he wanted to get a bus and send everybody back to Tuscaloosa who was late. We were that close, but Mal and the other coaches talked him out of it. They said you can't do that to 11 starters. He said the next night if anybody's late, we're definitely sending them back but nobody was late after that.

"What other plays do you remember?"

I was only at Alabama because of Coach Bryant. I've been asked that a lot. In 1976, I guess I was the first quarterback. I'm not saying I was that good, maybe it wasn't a strong year for quarterbacks. I had a good game when we played Auburn. We had the bowl game and then there was the Senior Bowl. Back then there was the Senior Bowl and the Hula Bowl. Of course one was in Hawaii and one in Mobile where I grew up. I got letters from both of them. Coach Bryant asked to see me and said, "You haven't called the Senior Bowl guys back yet". I said that I grew up in Mobile and I've never been to Hawaii. The farthest I've ever been is Tampa. He said, no you need to go to the Senior Bowl. He said I'm going to call this guy right now and you tell him that you're coming. I said yes sir. He knew that the Senior Bowl was the bowl that all the Scouts went to.

Another story is the day of the draft, I'm sitting there in my apartment in Tuscaloosa and the phone rings at 8:30 my time. This man said, do you have any problem signing? I said no sir and went back to sleep. About 12:30 the next day another call came from a guy from the Tuscaloosa News. He said congratulations, you've been signed in the first round! It's a lot different at the draft today with all the television and so forth.

"What else can you tell us about playing for Alabama?"

You don't understand how badly I stuttered. When I got in a ball game I wouldn't stutter, but at practice the guys would say our quarterback can't even talk! Coach Bryant would come down and listen to me talk. I had the fullback give the calls for me. I would signal him. You have to give the coaches credit for a lot of patience.

I remember the Maryland game. In those days you could only take so many players as a visiting team. So I had to punt. My first punt went straight up in the air. During our first two drives, Maryland played straight defense and they had Randy White, a super Hall of Famer. He went right up the middle. He was one of the fastest guys I had ever seen and it was 14 to 0 before you knew it. Then they started doing all this blitzing of the corners and then they shut us down. It was the fourth quarter and it was like 4th and 8 and I would be punting. I took off and I think I got a first down by very little. There were about 2 or 3 minutes left in the game. Had I not done that, I probably would not have played the rest of the year!

"How about that Notre Dame game?"

That was an amazing game. We missed an extra-point and they missed an extra-point, but they went for two and they made it. That was one heck of a game. Tom Clements was a great defensive end and an unbelievable player - 6'4" and 220. He would have been a perfect outside linebacker in the pros. He could outrun anybody, but he stumbled and we called him the "turf snake". He'd have a straight run and he'd stumble, but then he got up to his knees and kept going. I remember that's the only game I ever cried in the shower. When you lost coach never took it out on you. He would say that you did the best that you could. He was consoling.

He would come up to New York my first year with the Jets. Greg Gantt was our kicker. He was up there too, so we had the two of us from Alabama. The next year we had Marty. He would always call us when he would come up for the Hall of Fame dinner. They brought him up there a couple of other times too. We would talk for 30 or 40 minutes.

My dad was the most religious guy I'd ever seen and he knew the Bible inside and out. I wish I was more like him. My father and I didn't relate that much back in those days. I would say Coach Bryant was a father figure and Mal Moore also.

“Mal Moore was the architect of the wishbone wasn't he?”

If you look back at the history of how he did it, it's just remarkable. Coach Bryant had this passing offense with Joe Namath and Kenny Stabler, but they were going 6 and 5. I remember when they came out with the wishbone, I couldn't believe it. When they beat Southern California you could see what he did. He'd been coaching his whole life and to come out with a completely different offense. Then all of the success in the 70s and winning three national championships - the greatness of what he did what he thought and was something. It worked and I'm glad that I was a part of it.

Gary Rutledge “Rooster”, was kind of thought of as the passing quarterback and I was more the running quarterback. We didn't we didn't really throw that much when I was there. I remember after I left that Jeff Rutledge took over. Toward the end of that time it was much more of a passing offense - crossing patterns and stuff that we never did. Ours was just - ride the fullback, take two steps and step back. The passing game evolved a lot with the wishbone as time went on. In those days you were looking at one guy, it wasn't like the pros where you are reading everybody.

Johnny Davis was just amazing. I think he's the only guy who never lost. He would bounce off of one guy and go for another few yards. He was unbelievable. You would see him in the weight room and he had never lifted weights. He didn't have six abs, he had 16! I think he weighed 230. He would get on a bench press and bench more than me. He's doing like

225, but he'd say I don't lift weights. He was a funny man. He would get out there and play during the basketball games. He was just gifted.

Richard was a three-year starter at quarterback. In his sophomore year, Todd shared the quarterback position with Gary Rutledge.

In the Sugar Bowl at the end of the 1975 season, Todd threw for over 200 yards, and led Alabama to its first bowl victory in eight years. Alabama never lost an SEC game while Richard Todd was the starting quarterback.

He would end his college career throwing 16 TD while running for 1,254 yards and 16 TD.

The New York Jets drafted Todd in the first round of the 1976 Draft. The intention was for Todd to replace Joe Namath. Todd stated that playing on the same team with Namath was "a dream come true." After the 1976 season he was named the starter. In 1981, Todd led the Jets to their first winning record (10-5-1) since 1969. Todd played two seasons in New Orleans, as he replaced former Super Bowl winning, Kenny Stabler. Todd briefly returned to the Jets in 1986.

Todd finished his career with 1,610 completions in 2,967 attempts for 20,610 yards and 124 touchdowns. He also rushed for 932 yards and 14 touchdowns.

Johnny Davis – Fullback – 1974-1977

"Johnny why did you go to Alabama?"

First I was going to go to Auburn because my mother wanted me to go to Auburn and I was signed with them. They had a party planned for Saturday. Coach Bryant came by Friday night and took me for a ride. He said, "I'm not asking you, I'm telling you, you're going to Alabama." and I said, "yes sir, coach I've been waiting for you". That's why I went to Alabama. I went home and I told my mother and we used all that food that Auburn left for the party for a celebration for the signing with Alabama.

"You were a half back in high school is that right?"

No, I've never been a halfback my whole life because I was always big. I guess you would call me a running back-fullback in high school.

"Why did you want to play in the wishbone?"

Well I wanted to play for Coach Bryant in Alabama and the wishbone is what they were using. I wanted to play fullback in the wishbone because the fullback is the feature back in the wishbone and you can't beat that.

"Once Coach Bryant was not satisfied with how you had played. What happened that day?"

I think that we were doing an excessive celebration and Coach Bryant said always show your class. He made us go back to the dorm and ran all the coaches away. He said shut the dorm down. Sunday morning we had to play the whole game over, first-team offense against first-team defense. I almost quit that morning, but I'm glad I stayed. We had one player go home, but I think he came back. That was the toughest day of my life. Had I lived closer I probably would have walked home.

"What was your relationship with Coach Bryant?"

He was like a father figure to the players and I had a lot of respect for Coach Bryant and I didn't want to do anything to disappoint him or make him angry. So one day I was in practice and I was goofing off talking to the other players and I missed a block. Coach Bryant came up out of his tower and I said, where is he going who's he going to get. Guess what, he came and grabbed Johnny Davis right in the collar and said run that play again, run it again, run it again, run it again and I think I ran it at least 6 times and I never missed a block since. That changed my life.

"Another person you really admired was Wilbur Jackson"

He was the first African American to attend Alabama so he paved the way for all of us. I had a lot of respect for him. Wilbur was a great athlete. He had a lot of class and he had great speed. We loved Wilbur Jackson. I'm just thankful that he paved the way for myself and some other players to play at Alabama.

"What do you remember about the USC game?"

Alabama and USC had become a big rivalry. Coach Bryant put together a big back field and he put me at tail back and I scored from the tailback position. My first time playing that position I fumbled against the University of Maryland and I ended up on the wrong side line because I did not want to go up on the sideline with Coach Bryant. I'll never forget what he told me he said "do you know where you are?" I said I'm in the stadium. He said, "this is Alabama football and nobody fumbles at Alabama". I never fumbled again.

"Do you remember that touchdown against Auburn?"

I loved playing against Auburn because that was our biggest rival. Everybody wanted to have a good game against Auburn. I think it was the last game of the season and you wanted to leave a good taste in your mouth for the offseason.

"What did you say about running guys over?"

Auburn was a big rivalry against Alabama and we always wanted to have a good game against Auburn. It's the last game and it's an interstate rivalry. I just had a great game and someone asked me after the game from the media what did I think about playing against Auburn. I said I gave all those guys a free ride and I should have charged them!

"Any story that you would like to share about playing on the field, off the field, in the locker room with your teammates, with your coaches that you want to share? What about the Sugar Bowl game against Ohio State?"

That was the last college game Coach Bryant was against Woody Hayes. To finish your college career with that game was special. I had close to 100 yards and we won by about 30 points. To have a victory like that in your last college game was great. There's nothing like that because you want to finish strong. I went up to Coach Bryant's room after that game. Normally after a game you don't see your coach. You want to go hang out with the other players and your friends, but I did go up to see Coach Bryant to tell him thanks for having me play at Alabama. That was a great moment. He wished me good luck and told me that I should have a good future in football. I'll never forget that.

"Coach Bryant called you the greatest fullback that he had ever coached"

Well, I needed a lot of coaching, but Alabama had a lot of great fullbacks. Billy Jackson was a great fullback. A lot of great players played at Alabama so for him to say that that was a great honor at that time. I'm really appreciative of that.

"Any other memories that you would like to share?"

I was in a passing game and one time I went down the middle of the field so they double-covered me. They fired that defensive coordinator.

"They called you the bull at Alabama is that right?"

I'm not sure how I got the name I guess somebody at practice said he's running like a bull and that just stuck and it became my nickname.

The last thing that Coach Bryant told me when I was I was playing for Tampa Bay. I was playing the piano Coach Bryant told me you need to quit playing that piano and play some football. At Alabama the most important thing for me was Johnny Davis, Ozzie Newsome and I marched at graduation. That was real important for all of us and I think Coach Bryant was proud of us. My mom was proud of us. That was a blessing.

One thing I would say about the wishbone was we had some great offensive lineman. They would block sometimes 3 defensive players. You got eyes on the outside and that made it easy for Johnny Davis to get five yards per carry. It was a great offense.

While at Alabama, Johnny rushed for 2,519 yards and 21 touchdowns. Coach Bryant called him "the best fullback I've ever coached". Davis led in rushing in three of his four seasons at Alabama. He was named to the Alabama Team of the Decade 1970's, 2nd Team UPI All-America Team 1977, 1st Team All-SEC 1977, 2nd Team All-SEC 1976 and 2nd Team All-SEC 1975. As a senior he was invited to the 1978 Senior Bowl. Johnny and Ozzie Newsome were roommates throughout their college careers and still remain friends.

Johnny was drafted in round 2 in 1978 by the Tampa Bay Buccaneers. In 1981, he played for the San Francisco 49ers, where he won a Super Bowl XVI ring. He averaged a touchdown every 13 times he carried the ball for the 49ers. In 1982, he signed with the Cleveland Browns and played alongside Ozzie Newsome.

He was a tough inside runner and considered one of the best blocking fullbacks in NFL history. He played in 119 regular season games, started 32, and had 15 rushing TD's, 1,094 rushing yards, 22 receptions, and 106 receiving yards in his professional career.

Described by those who know him as "unselfish, hard-working and always smiling, He is a powerful blocker and an excellent kickoff coverage man."

Ozzie Newsome – Wide Receiver – 1974-1977

"Ozzie why did you choose to go to Alabama?"

I had an opportunity to go to some schools that I could have caught a lot of balls. I went to Alabama for the opportunity to win a National Championship and play in a major bowl game.

"Ozzie what are your feelings about the passing game with the wishbone offense?"

You were almost guaranteed one on one coverage because the way they had to load up to stop majority of the time you got one on one coverage.

"Did you ever envision being an All-American?"

I didn't even envision playing at Alabama. When you get there, all you want to do is be a part of the team. I had some success early, I was able to start as a freshman and things just built from there.

"How was it playing with Jeff Rutledge and Richard Todd?"

They are both good athletes. Richard could beat you with his feet as well as his arms. Jeff was really smart. I think what set them both apart was the ability to put the ball in the right place.

“What was your relationship like with Coach Bryant?’

Like all of the other guys that played, the lessons that he taught us while we were there are the lessons that we are living right now. A lot of the things that he taught me as a player alone a lot of the things that I utilize as a GM in Baltimore right now. Martin Luther King asked for opportunity and Coach Bryant gave me opportunity.

“In your junior year you played a little bit of tight end”

Well it was all about getting the best guys on the field. At Alabama all you wanted to do was have the opportunity to play with some good young receivers that were coming along. In order to get the best 11 players on the field, he wanted me to play tight end.

“What is the legacy of the wishbone and how it has affected the game today?”

If you look at Auburn's offense, that's basically the wishbone that they're running. Everything comes off the play pass and if you get the running game going you can get some great plays.

“Do you remember the Maryland game?”

I was green at that point. We were using the receivers to carry the plays in. I took the second play in the second game of the season. I've been living there for 20 years and I happen to have a picture on my phone by someone who was at the game. I caught my very first pass in college football in that game and all I want to say is Roll Tide!

Coach Bryant called him, "the greatest end in Alabama history. A total team player, fine blocker, outstanding leader, great receiver with concentration, speed, hands”.

Newsome started for all 4 years of his college career, nicknamed "The Wizard of Oz". He made the College Football All-America Team in 1977 and assisted the Crimson Tide to a 42 and 6 overall record during his four seasons. Newsome amassed 102 receptions for 2,070 receiving yards and 16 touchdowns. Ozzie was named the Alabama Player of the Decade for the 1970s. He was two-time All-SEC in 1976 and 1977, and named SEC Lineman of the Year in 1977. In 1994, Newsome was elected to the College Football Hall of Fame.

Newsome was drafted in the first round of the 1978 NFL draft by the Cleveland Browns. Ozzie went to the Pro Bowl in 1981, 1984 and 1985. In 1986, Newsome won the Ed Block Courage Award for playing with injuries, and in 1990 won the Byron "Whizzer" White NFL Man of the Year Award for his community service.

Newsome finished his career with 662 receptions and 7,980 yards, both Cleveland franchise records, and 47 touchdowns, fifth all-time. In 1999 Newsome was inducted into the Pro Football Hall of Fame.

Newsome was a front office executive with the Cleveland Browns from 1991 until their relocation to Baltimore in 1996; he then became an executive with the Baltimore Ravens. On November 22, 2002, Newsome was named the first general manager of the Ravens, making him the first African-American to occupy that position in the NFL until 2018.

Tony Nathan- Running Back – 1975-1978

"What was your impression of Alabama running the wishbone?"

I didn't really think about it. I was more concerned about who I could play for and who the coach would be and I wasn't really impressed by the other schools that tried to recruit me. If you can run the football, you can run the football anywhere so the offense didn't really matter to me. It was more so about the coach that cared about me and I cared about him. Coach Bryant cared about me and that's why I came to Alabama.

"What were your thoughts after the 1977 USC game?"

You're playing the top dog in the country and you've got to give your best effort and whatever the outcome is you know that you left it all on the field.

"What about the 78 sugar bowl with Ohio State?"

All I know is I like getting in the end zone and they called me "Touchdown Tony" and I guess it stuck. I enjoyed playing with the best. That's how you get to show that you can compete with the best.

"What about the 79 sugar bowl with Penn State?"

That game was very physical. Bruce Clark and Matt Millen were both defensive tackles. They were very physical, so I'm glad we won. If it hadn't been for that goal line stand we might not have won.

“What was your relationship like with Coach Bryant?”

In the beginning, being a young man away from home my mom said, I'm trusting you with my child. My experience with him was he taught me how to respect others, on and off the field. In the first scrimmage I scored on a punt return and I did a little dance in the end zone. Coach came up to me and tapped me on the shoulder and said, son we have no lightning bolts around here. It took me a minute and I said, okay Coach I won't show it no more. He said, do yourself a favor and act like you've been there before and give the ball back to the official. That let me know at that point who he was and what he was going to do for me as a person and I respected him for it.

“What was the next important lesson that you learned from him?”

He was the same on the field as off the field. He knew how to read people and how important you were to the team itself. He was straight up about whether you could play for him or whether you couldn't play for him. If you couldn't play for him he would say, you'll get your education, but you'll never play for me. He stuck by what he said and what he told you and you had to keep your word because the only thing a man has is his word.

“Why do you think the wishbone was so successful?”

It all starts with the guys up front. If they are as good or better than the guys they're facing that's the beginning of it. If the quarterback and the running back are worth their salt, when they're given the opportunity you take advantage of the opportunity. It's one of the type of offenses that eventually will take control of the game itself. It's the type of offense that you will run the football and you're going to be physical with people. To play it you had to be physical.

"Did you feel like you were part of something special?"

There wasn't very many schools running the wishbone. If you're running the 'I', the guy in the back is going to get the ball most of the time, but in the wishbone they don't know which way you're going to go. You can start one way and go back the other and you still have two backs you can deal with. It's deceiving at times but in the end when you decide that you got to run the football you just say, here we come and we're coming.

"What would you describe as the legacy of the wishbone?"

There was respect for it across the country because of the way we ran it. I guess you could say we almost perfected it. When you think about the way some people run a two back offense and the open offense they're running nowadays, they're doing the same thing. The quarterback is keeping the ball and sometimes you're bringing a receiver around and you pitch it. It still has a big impact on the way people are running offenses nowadays but it's just different formations.

"What is a favorite memory that you have?"

I had to tell coach that I was going to drop out of school. He didn't take it too well, but you have to go on and do what you got to do with your life. I got drafted and got married. I played a few years in Miami and had a family. I did make him the promise that one day I would finish college and it took me quite a few years but we got it done. When you give a man your word to do something, that's the one thing that you have to do. I gave him my word that I would do it and I ended up doing that for him.

In his four seasons with the Crimson Tide, Nathan rushed for 1,997 yards, with 29 touchdowns. Also excelling as a kick returner, he finished his college career with 30 touchdowns and 3,362 all-purpose yards, including a 10.9 average in yards per punt return.

Nathan was the Dolphins' starting running back in Super Bowl XVII and Super Bowl XIX.

He finished his nine NFL seasons with 3,543 yards rushing, 383 receptions for 3,592 yards, and 32 touchdowns, 16 each rushing and receiving. He retired from playing in 1988, and became an assistant to Don Shula. He became the Dolphins' running backs coach in 1993. He served under Tony Dungy as the running backs coach for the Tampa Bay Buccaneers from 1996 to 2001.

From 2003 to 2005, Nathan was the running backs coach at Florida International University. He was inducted into the Senior Bowl Hall of Fame in 2006. He returned to the NFL coaching ranks as the Baltimore Ravens' running backs coach. In 2008 Nathan was hired as the San Francisco 49ers' running backs coach.

Major Ogilvie – Running Back – 1977-1980

"How did you end up at Alabama?"

That's not an easy question to answer because there's a lot of factors there. Early on I was privileged to play with a lot of successful programs, and of course Alabama was an extremely successful program. Like a lot of us who played for Coach Bryant, there was that certain attachment that went with the knowledge of him and respect. When that opportunity came, there wasn't any hesitation on my part.

"What was one of your most memorable recruiting moments?"

I was playing in high school and we had a really good football team, but back then recruiting didn't really start until your senior year. We won the state championship in that year so recruiting was kind of challenging because I was on a good team. The thing that I remember the most is when I visited Alabama. There was a dinner that I went to with my parents and Coach Bryant said, "Don't come here unless you want to play to win a National Championship", and that's always resonated with me.

"What do you remember about the first time you met him?"

I had met Coach Bryant when I was little. Actually signing day my senior year was my birthday, so we went down to the university and I kind of slipped out of there and went down to Coach Bryant's office and talked to him a little bit. I said, I'd like to see one of your championship rings and he put his hand out and it showed it to me and I remember that.

"You're considered one of the legends of the wishbone offense how do you feel about that?"

Well the wishbone was a great team offense. It created a lot of discipline for our team and it fit Coach Bryant to a 'T' because we were all about the team winning. That's the way I see my role. I was very fortunate to have been down there during that time with the teammates and the coaches. Coach Bryant was in his 21st, 22nd and 23rd years at the University, so there was a lot of tradition in place for us to have fun. We did back then, but they didn't talk about the offensive line the way they do today. We were running backs and we carried the ball so you would get your name in the paper, but the wishbone was a great team offense and it was perfect for us.

"The wishbone uses a lot of running backs. What was so special about your role?"

My role as a running back was to carry the ball and I wasn't supposed to fumble. As a running back in the wishbone you had to be able to block. People think of it as a power football kind of offense, but the way we ran the wishbone, there was a lot of finesse involved. There weren't that many other teams that ran the wishbone, so there was a certain amount of surprise that teams would see. It was a lot quicker offense than most teams. It was a real advantage for us because other teams didn't run it. We could surprise them. Through the years with Coach Moore, we had some variations that gave us advantages - like the double wing that we ran against Arkansas. It was a great team offense. All our team members that made the cut with him had the opportunity to play, so that made it fun for all of us. Everybody had an opportunity to contribute and so we had a great time as a team.

“What was your experience in playing with the tear away jerseys?”

I was there when tear away jerseys were used and when they were ended. During my freshman and sophomore years, if you had a tear away jersey and the official said he couldn't read your number, we had a way to handle it. Our guards or tackles would have some on the field so we could just reach and pull out our jersey and put another one on. But my junior year the officials said if they couldn't read your number, you had to come out and you had to call a timeout. So late in the season during my junior year, there was a team that took advantage of that. We would be tackled and they would tear our jerseys on the ground. So that was kind of the beginning of the end. During my freshman year toward the end of the season, my grandmother called my mother and said that my hair looked bushy and it was about time for me to get a haircut. She asked me what I was doing sticking my hands in the pants of the other player! She didn't see the whole thing because our guards kept the jerseys in the back of their pants. She was very much relieved when she understood. That was a real advantage for us early on because the type of tackling had changed and you were using your arms a lot more and shoulders, so the tear away jersey was a good advantage for us.

“Tell us about the 1977 Southern Cal game”

Well we played at the coliseum and they were ranked first and we were second. We won the game and it was huge for us. We had played Nebraska, I think 3 weeks before that and they had a great team. We walked out of the coliseum with a tremendous amount of confidence and we were going to have a great team that year and we did.

"Was there any particular play in that game that you remember?"

No, because we played in one big game after another. That was a national TV game and there was always a lot of interest. That year I played left half and the next year I played right half. In the middle of the second quarter the coach put in the second unit and I was running the ball. We had made a nice gain and I hit the ground pretty hard and the ball popped out. Thank goodness the official called me down because it was a key spot during the game. We needed to keep the drive going and we did. I remember that play.

"What about the 1978 game against Washington, when Steadman pitched to the left? "

It was a long plane ride up there - 6 hours. We left on a Thursday. It was kind of wet that day and Washington had a good team in 1978. I think four of the teams that we played we're ranked high in the beginning of the year so we had to be good the early part of the year which was not typical for us. The Washington game was key for us and we just barely got by. That play when Steadman pitched to me and I made a touchdown was a key play in the game. They had gained the momentum late and we needed to have more points than they did at the end.

"The third quarter of the 1978 national championship game against Penn State in the Sugar Bowl you ran for a touchdown. Tell us about that play."

The one team that we played that matched up against the wishbone as well as any team we ever played by far was Penn State. That was the toughest football game I had ever played in. Any player that played in that game would tell you the same thing. It was a hard-hitting, demanding game. There were a lot of big plays in that game. They had 2 tackles that could read the belly play, we called it. If the fullback doesn't get the ball it presents problems for the wishbone because you're trying to read that tackle and get him out of the way. We couldn't do that with Bruce Clark and Matt Millen because they were on both sides of the ball. If a team had one good tackle, you could just go to the other side, but they had two that were very agile and very strong. If you watch that play, it's not a typical wishbone play. I think it was Bruce Clark - when Jeff put the ball in the belly of the fullback, he took it out thinking Bruce was going to tackle our fullback. It was all Jeff could do to get the ball out and put it in the air so I could catch it. Of course that left the end open, but we had an end out there that made a critical block. We had a little crease so we could get in. That was a big play for us. There were a lot of great plays in that game. We had a turnover at one point in the second quarter and the Penn State guy was going to go for a touchdown. It was a tough, tough ball game.

"Do you remember anything about the Auburn game that year?"

The '79 team was the best football team that I was ever a part of. We had a great offensive line. A lot of things were in place. We just had some great players on that team. We weren't really talented, but we were a great team. Typical of all Auburn games, there were some great plays. Auburn was actually ahead of us late in the game. We got the ball on our 2 yard line and had to drive the ball 98 yards in order to win. I think they were ahead of us. Another thing about that drive was we had just started it and made a couple of plays. I think we had gotten out to the 10-yard line. Steadman was running the triple option and I was the pitchman. Steadman got hit kind of funny, right when he was trying to pitch. The ball went straight down on the ground and thank goodness it popped up in my hands so we were lucky that day.

"How about the Sugar Bowl?"

It didn't start out too well for us. They kicked it to us and we had a very good offense, but they got the ball within our 20-yard line and made a field goal. They hadn't gotten savvy about us yet, so we got a drive going in the first quarter. A big part of that game was that they had a very small, agile defensive line, but they had big linebackers that were really quick. They could cover a lot of area, so Coach Moore put the halfbacks in a double wing. That gave us an advantage speed-wise. The halfback could get down to the linebacker. The linebacker was responsible for taking care of the pitch. Most of our offense that day, particularly the first two quarters into the third quarter, we used the triple part of the wishbone offense. It was pitch to the halfback. We made some long runs, but they made some adjustments in the second half. They started covering out there. That was a fun game. Coach Bryant won his first national championship against Arkansas in 1961. The 6th National Championship was against Arkansas in 1979 and both were in the Sugar Bowl as well.

"Which national championship team is the most memorable to you?"

Both of them! We just had so many good experiences with Coach Bryant playing in Alabama. We played in so many big ball games. We had some great teammates. Our practices at times could be pretty challenging and Coach Bryant made it that way. I wouldn't want to single out one or the other because both of them meant a lot and we reached our goals.

"You had so much talent around you. What was it like playing with all that talent?"

I never looked at us as having that much talent. I thought we were a good team because we had been molded to work together. Our practices could be very challenging. When your number was up, you couldn't make it through those practices without your teammate patting you on the rear end and telling you to hang in there. You would be doubling over just crying to take another step.

“What about Shealy as a quarterback?”

He was a great wishbone quarterback. He really was. All of us had that desire to win and all of us played together really well. If you talk about the quarterbacks that I played with, you had Jack O’Rear, Jeff Rutledge, Steadman, Don Jacobs, Walter Lewis and Alan Gray - your true wishbone quarterbacks. They were geared more toward the running part of the wishbone. Of course Jeff was a great passer, so all of them put different pressures on the defense from a different standpoint. Steadman was a great runner, particularly when he got on the corner. He was more of a running back quarterback then say Jeff was or even Jack O’Rear he was pretty fast too.

“What's your favorite memory playing football for Alabama?”

I can't separate them. I mean it was four years. Every one of them was great, playing for Coach Bryant. All of us count our blessings every day for that and all the things he did for us. Frankly, that impact continues on our lives.

“What's your favorite Coach Bryant memory?”

My junior year we had played Tennessee in Birmingham. The first half was pretty rough for us. The second half we came out and won the game, but I got hurt. It was a pretty serious thing and I had to go to the hospital. I had been in the hospital for 3 weeks and it was really uncomfortable for me to move. The week of the LSU game, Coach Bryant called me up. At that time the telephones were in the hall and it was about 11 on Wednesday night before the LSU game. The nurse came running in and said Coach Bryant is on the phone! I just got out of bed and he asked me how I was feeling and at first I said fine. Then I thought I better prop that up a little bit and I said good. He called me Thursday at 6 in the morning and asked how are you? and I hadn't run or walk. In 3 weeks he called me Thursday at lunch and asked me did I feel like walking out to practice. Coach Bryant was the kind of person that you just said, "yes sir". So I was walking out and he pulls up in his little golf cart and he asked me, "Do you feel like running a few plays?" I said yes sir, and Coach Goostree put about a mile of tape on me. I came back out there and ran five or six plays. Coach Bryant came up after practice and said, "Boy you look good out there today". I went back to the hospital and he called me that night to ask me how I was feeling. I came out and ran five plays on Friday. After the practice he tells me he wants me to go to Baton Rouge with the team, but not to dress. The weather was horrible. It had been raining for a couple of days. Saturday morning he called me and asked how I'm feeling. That was a night game. We get to the stadium and back then it was customary for the players to load their gear Friday afternoon. Well of course I didn't load anything, but when I got to my locker there were my pads. Coach Bryant came in and said it would help us more by getting dressed. So we were getting ready for warm-ups and he asked me if I felt like going out and catching punts. I was in the end zone catching punts and Coach Goostree, who was our trainer, waddled down to talk to me. He said, "You're looking spry tonight". Later on he came and said we may play you tonight. The third time he waddled up and said, "I don't want to scare you, but I think you're going to start"! So that's my favorite Coach Bryant story. I played the whole game and we won 3 to 0. It rained all night and it was a nasty situation.

Coach Goostree was such a key part of our success at Alabama. He was in charge of getting us well and making sure we could play and contribute. Of course you hardly played in college where there wasn't something wrong with you.

"So what do you think is your legacy in Alabama football history?"

The success of the players in the 30s, 40s, 50s and the 60s - it's all been a part of Alabama football. We are a part of it and like a lot of them, we got to do some pretty unique things and play for a really unique coach.

"You hear guys who played for Coach Bryant say there's not a day that goes by that they don't think about something he told us or taught us," he said in an interview with Sports Illustrated. "That's true."

While at Alabama, Major rushed for 1,718 yards and scored 25 touchdowns. He also received for 1. Major was an All-SEC First Team selection and an Academic All-American in 1979. He was selected as the Most Valuable Player in both the 1980 Sugar Bowl and 1981 Cotton Bowl. He was Captain of the 1980 team and holds the distinction of being named to the All-Decade Team for both the 1970s and 1980s.

Dwight Stephenson – Center – 1976-1979

"How were you recruited at Alabama?"

Two other guys on my football team we're highly-recruited so the University of Alabama came down and they wanted those two guys. My high school coach talked to them and said you have to look at Dwight Stephenson. He's just getting into football and is not a bad player, it seems like he has some potential. They said we'll take Dwight Stephenson as well. All three of us got scholarships, but those two guys decided they were not going to go to Alabama. I wanted to play for a very top notch program and Coach Bryant so that was something that was very exciting to me.

"What was it like meeting Coach Bryant for the first time?"

He was a guy that was well-respected and everybody loved and thought a lot of him so to meet him was really very special. He seemed to be very interested in me as a person and interested in my family. I thought a guy that is really that big that made time for me was something that made me feel special.

"What do you remember about running the wishbone offense?"

I loved it. It was a very aggressive offense, so that's the only offense that I wanted to play in. Being able to knock people back really helped me develop my ability as an offensive lineman.

"Which was the most memorable national championship?"

The first one had to be the biggest one for me it was just something to play against Penn State in the Sugar Bowl. Coach Bryant was on one side and Coach Paterno on the other. That was an awesome feeling to see two of the best coaches that played the game coaching against one another. I felt like I was in football heaven. That was the most memorable to me.

"Do you think that the wishbone can be used today?"

I think that the wishbone can be seen in the pros today. Guys are doing the wildcat. Some variation of the wishbone will be back at some point. I think it's a great offense. I really enjoyed the wishbone.

"What did you enjoy most about the wishbone?"

I enjoyed being aggressive and we did variations on it. We would have passes and so on. It was just coming off the football and knocking people back and making 2 or 3 yards and then all of a sudden you would make a touchdown.

"What did you take from these experiences in moving forward?"

When I got to the pros it was easier for me to compete because of what had happened at Alabama. I was better prepared on our fundamentals and the things that coach Bryant put in our heads. Because of running the wishbone I was prepared as any offensive lineman in the NFL. You don't want to be retreating, you want to be running ahead and blocking and knocking people back. The wishbone prepared us very well for that.

"How did Coach Bryant affect your life?"

Coach Bryant was the right guy at the right time in my life. He taught us about football, but it was really about life - not giving up when things are going to be difficult - tough love. We learned all of that from Coach Bryant. There were other coaches that were special as well - Ken Donahue and Jack Rutledge. We had some great assistant coaches such as Mal Moore. I had quality people around me and they were committed to making Alabama the best team in the country. We didn't lose a Southeastern Conference game for 3 years and we won back-to-back national championships. We were a team so it wasn't just one player that carried the team. We were a unit - we all worked really well together.

"So what is your favorite football memory?"

Probably when we played the University of Tennessee in Birmingham. I think we fell behind so before I knew it they were up on us 17 to nothing. We went to the locker room and Coach Bryant said, okay guys we got them right where we want them. What he did was psychological. He let us know that we had better get out there and get it together. We went back out there that second half and we scored the points that we needed to win. We scored 24 points and I don't think they scored again. We knew that we had to win that game or Sunday morning we would be out there practicing again.

Coach Bryant called Stephenson the best center he ever coached, and described him as "a man among children". He was the team's starting center from 1977 to 1979, and was a member of Alabama's back-to-back national championship teams of 1978 and 1979. He was a two-time second-team All-American. "His speed, his foot quickness, was off the chart," said Mike Brock, a former Alabama lineman. "You couldn't compare it to other people who played at that time. There was no way for defenses to deal with him”.

Stephenson was drafted by Don Shula and the Miami Dolphins in the second round of the 1980 NFL Draft. Stephenson was universally recognized as the premier center in the NFL.

With the exceptionally explosive Stephenson as offensive captain, the Dolphins offensive line gave up the fewest sacks in the NFL for a record six straight seasons, from 1982 to 1987.

He was the starting center in the Dolphins' two Super Bowl appearances: Super Bowl XVII and Super Bowl XIX. In 1985, Stephenson was the recipient of the NFL Man of the Year Award for "outstanding community service and playing excellence."

Stephenson was voted as an All-Pro five consecutive times from 1983 to 1987. He was selected to play on five Pro Bowl squads over the same span. He was named AFC Offensive Lineman of the Year He started at center in the AFC Championship Game three times, in 1982, 1984, and 1985.

Steadman Shealy – Quarterback – 1977-1979

"How did you come to be recruited at Alabama?"

Well my family was from Alabama and my sister was a bear girl. I spent a day of prayer asking God, where do you want me to go? Alabama had signed the top five quarterbacks in the state the year before. Mississippi State, Auburn and Georgia were all saying, you can come in and be the number two quarterback. Alabama said we want you to come but no promises. That's just where the Lord led me to go. I'm in my living room. We had just played in the state finals against Major Ogilvie and his team. That next week I had Doug Barfield, who was Auburn's head coach in my living room. Vince Dooley, who was Georgia's head coach, was out in the car. As I'm talking with Coach Barfield, my mom opens the door and goes, Coach Bryant's on the phone. I said okay. He said, "What's your problem? If you'll commit to Alabama I'll come down and personally sign you." I didn't commit that night and I said, "Coach I'll get back with you". I really did some hard praying.

"Had you met him before that?"

I met him on my recruiting trip. It was awesome.

"What was your take on the wishbone offense?"

It was the perfect offense for me with my size and speed. It was a dream offense. When I played, the quarterbacks got to call their plays and audibles anytime they wanted. You would read your way out. Everything started with the quarterback. If you stunk, the play didn't work. If you executed, you're going to make 8 yards. I played a lot as a sophomore and a junior. We had two quarterbacks, Jeff Rutledge was the passer and I was the runner. It really worked out, it and was just an awesome offense for me.

“But you tore your knee up pretty bad?”

That was another miracle. The doctor said I also had a severe infection, so I went from 190 to 160 pounds. I would go to the pool to do my water rehab and everybody would kind of laugh at me because I had such skinny legs. I remember the week before they were going to allow me to start practicing, they said I had to get to 125 degrees in flexion in my knee. I would tie my leg up every night and they made me a brace. I didn't sleep for a week and was in constant pain. But in a week's time, I got to 125 degrees of flexion and I was allowed to practice. We were out playing Missouri and I was standing near Coach Bryant and things weren't going well. I'd only had a week's practice and had missed the Nebraska game. Jeff's the starter. Things were now going well and Coach Bryant always liked to play other people. I only had a week's practice and Coach Bryant said “now I'm going to put Steadman in”. Coach Moore said, “Coach you don't need to do that” and Coach Bryant said a few things as only he could do. The first thing you know I'm in. I gained nine yards and thought I was going to die when I got hit because I hadn't been hit in so long. But I took them down for a field goal. I was okay the rest of the year and we went on to become national champions.

“There was a famous play in the 1978 Washington Huskies game, tell me about it”

It was a tremendous play because it was a very close game. If their wide receiver hadn't dropped a touchdown pass, they would have beaten us.

But let me talk about Major Ogilvie for a moment. I remember the big drive against Auburn. We were down 18 to 17 and Coach Bryant benched the first-team offense to start the 4th quarter and put in the second team. We are all foaming at the mouth because we had to win. We're number one in the country and we're undefeated. We're playing Auburn and things just fell apart in the first quarter. So the first play I ride the fullback and the ball slipped out of my hand! Thank goodness it bounced up to Major Ogilvie and he gained 15 yards, then we went down the field and got to the 8-yard line. I ran the option left and cut in and went in and scored. Then we scored on the two-point conversion. We beat Auburn 25 to 18 and we went on to be national champions (1979).

“What was so awesome about scoring in that game?”

Well growing up in Alabama, you realized the importance of beating Auburn. I would get phone calls from all over the world and get letters about it. But even more important than that that was our next step in the goal of a perfect season and being number one. In the three years that I played, we were 34 and 2. We never lost an SEC game. It was all about the national title. That helped us get there. Of course I tell people all the time that I had the greatest group of guys - the greatest line.

“Besides that game which is the most memorable to you?”

I think the Arkansas game, because that was our bowl game. That was a game that we had to win. We came out with something very unique in the wishbone. It was called a “double wing”. All we would do is take the back. We still ran the wishbone but it looked different. Arkansas was in a base defense the whole game. They didn't know what to do with it and we just executed. It was just one of those games where you do everything right. The only thing I did badly was out of the end zone someone was open and I over threw it. But I said, if I can overthrow you, you weren't running fast enough! But otherwise it was one of those games of great execution. We won and then we were crowned unanimous national champions. When you grow up in Alabama, that's your dream. We had won the National Championship the year before and we made a pact that we were going to go undefeated and be number one. We did. When you set a goal like that and it happens, you're like wow isn't this fun?

“What was the fan base like back then?”

The fans expected it, but more importantly we expected it. There's nobody that we ever played where we ever doubted that we were going to win. When we walked on the field, we felt like we were the best. We had the best defense in the country so we practiced at times during game preparation. Everybody asks me, who was the greatest defense you ever played against? - my own! I played Nebraska and USC twice. Penn State was just a little bit below our defense. It was amazing. We had a great defense and Coach Bryant would always say, “You win on defense and kicking”. He was right. The wishbone controlled the game, so you kept your defense off the field. It's about time of possession. You eat up the clock and grind it out. It's hard-nosed, jaw to mouth football.

“Do you think the wishbone offense was the right offense for that era, because not a lot of people were running it?”

Because of the rules at the time – yes. When the rules changed, where the lineman could extend their hands, then no more wishbone. Everybody went to the west coast offense and others. The 70s, I think was the greatest time in all of football. It was unbelievable. Definitely Coach Bryant was a genius. What most people don't realize is that the wishbone made everybody tough. When everybody would say, who's going to start in the fall? - I would say, who's left standing? It was a very intense go-get-'em offense. Today it's more about finesse - it's just a different game.

"What about the practices?"

Well we hit a lot. We got after it. We called it, the best against the best. The hh's were the headhunters. The number one defense against the reds, the number one offense. We would go against each other. There were more fireworks than any football game I've ever been a part of. It was the most intense atmosphere to be a part of. That's why when we were playing USC out in the coliseum – they're number one in the county - we beat them and I'll never forget. I think we were down 6 to 3 at halftime or maybe three to nothing. Coach Bryant walks in and says, "all right guys, we got them where we want them". We went out and to smash them in the second half.

"Do you think the wishbone offense could work in today's game?"

No. When I played, we played 50 people in the first half and now it's a pro mentality. You can't do that. It's just too intense, too physical. The competition at Alabama was so great. Every practice meant something because you knew the guy behind you could take your place. How well you played in the game would determine how much you played. That's why I got to play a lot as a sophomore and a junior. If you move the ball, then Coach Bryant was going to let you play. It was an atmosphere of competition that's just hard to imagine. I remember seeing guys being on the 3rd team the next week because they didn't play well. Coach Bryant would fire coaches during the game, but of course they would be rehired. Games were so intense. It's the most amazing offense from a quarterback standpoint. We always read our way out. We would leave the tackles unblocked so we never went to the strong side. I never understood why defenses didn't realize what we were doing. When I counted six to the right, I always went to left. If I counted six to the left, I always went right.

"What is your favorite football memory at Alabama?"

I would have to say scoring the winning touchdown against Auburn to win the game. That is definitely my favorite memory. We were a better football team. We had worked all year and we were undefeated and number one. All our dreams were right there, but it all disintegrated in the third quarter when we fumbled 5 times. The next thing you know, we're down 18 to 17, but we marched it 82 yards. I was fortunate enough to score the winning touchdown and that preserved our undefeated season. We went on to beat Arkansas in the Sugar Bowl.

"Did you ever carry the coach on your shoulders after the game?"

We did it after the sugar bowl. Of course I didn't do it - that's for the bigger guys. Because Coach Bryant was a big man, he usually didn't like it, but he was okay because it was the national championship.

"What was Coach Bryant like and what was your relationship?"

I was one of the most fortunate people in the world because I got to know Coach Bryant personally. He would always say, "I want to take a walk with the quarterbacks". I got to know him when I was coaching for him for 3 years and then I co-hosted the "Coach Bryant Show" his last year. I was the first person to know that he was going to retire. We're up in Birmingham taping the show and he walked in after getting beaten by Southern Mississippi. He walked in and said, "Steadman, I'm going to retire. I feel like I'm losing my edge". Then I had to do the show and I was shook up because I couldn't believe it. We just had a great relationship. I was so fortunate. I would go over to see Mrs. Bryant and we would read the Bible together. She was just precious. What was so funny though is she would say, "you know Paul" and I would get goosebumps because you never called him that or bear, you always called him Coach Bryant.

"So what was it like after being a quarterback and coaching with Coach Bryant?"

That was just tremendous because it made me understand what went on in his staff meetings. One thing that Coach Bryant would do was, we called it "trolling". He would just see what coach was going to bite. He'd make his point, because Coach Bryant would "coach the coaches" and then we would coach the players. At that stage Coach Bryant's power was that he determined who played. He wasn't calling plays per se at that stage in his career. Coaching the wishbone was easy, but the defenses were getting a little bit more complicated. We had to run some variations at the end, so we had predetermined reads. We had a little more speed and we were beginning to get faster backs, things of that nature. The defenses were different. One of the great stories about the wishbone is when I came in as a freshman we had just gotten beaten by Missouri 21 to 0 on national TV and we were so embarrassed. They would come out with the "gap 8" and we thought, that's the defense that's going to shut down the wishbone forever. What was great about Coach Moore, who was also named the wishbone wizard, came up with different plays that we would run against the gap 8. So we would never be caught unaware. We couldn't make the adjustments when Missouri did that and we were just shut down. Everybody was coming up with some wild strategy. That's why we had our rule - you don't run to the 6 side, you just count and you had to know your read. If you did, it always worked as long as you executed. It was the greatest offense ever - it was a man's offense.

At Alabama Shealy rushed for 1393 yards and 17 touchdowns. He passed for 924 yards. Shealy hosted The Bear Bryant Show in 1982 and served as a graduate assistant in the football program.

Billy Jackson – Fullback – 1977-1980

What led you to play for Alabama?"

It was a really easy choice for me. In high school we ran the wishbone, so I was used to that and I played both halfback and fullback in high school. Coach Bryant came down my junior year and he came up and shook my hand. I was just trembling. He said, I heard about you and I got a scholarship waiting for you, just don't get hurt. I was sold after that.

In my sophomore year I didn't start. I happened to be in the game and there was an opening and I just ran. Everybody kidded me about that and it was the longest run I had in my college career.

"You played in that undefeated team in 1979?"

In 1979 I played fullback in my sophomore year and I went to half back my junior year. The biggest game I had was the Sugar Bowl.

The Arkansas game was the first game that I played where I was really healthy. We had a little layoff and I was able to take a week off. We came back and I think that was probably the best game that I had in 1979.

"What are your thoughts about your relationship with Coach Bryant?"

I think I had a very good relationship. When you go out there and do what you're supposed to do, you won't have any problems with Coach Bryant. I was a person who always went to class and I never missed curfew. I always tried to do everything I was supposed to do on the field. I think one of the most memorable moments I had was when I was in the pros, this was within 12 hours before coach Bryant passed away, I sat in his office and talked to him for about 30 minutes. The next morning I woke up and found out that he had had a heart attack and had passed away so that always stuck with me.

"Do you remember some of that conversation?"

I can remember that he didn't want to retire because when he would go back to Arkansas he would see in the graveyard his parents and all these people who worked until they were in their 80s. They were all farmers so they didn't really know about retiring. I think he knew that he probably didn't have much longer. If he ever did something wrong he never had a problem admitting it. He would never criticize a player. He would say, I didn't prepare well enough, but on Mondays the players would take the brunt for the loss.

I was fortunate because we only lost four games the whole time I was there. I was on two national championship teams. I played fullback my sophomore year and I played halfback my junior year then I went back to fullback.

It was hard at Alabama. When you went to the locker room after the game and he said "NT", that meant no time. You might have 75 plays straight and you don't even stop. Coach Bryant said, "Billy I wish that I had redshirted you, your freshman year". I never told him, but I thought to myself, coach, I wish you had.

I got hit and I was laying on the ground for about 30 seconds and I got up and I was walking over to the sideline. The first person I saw when I went over there was Coach Bryant. He looked over and said, Jackson are you alright? I said, yes coach. He was the type of guy that you would never say, no I can't do it. He really made an impact on my life. He taught me the will to win. Like now, I'm determined to win. I don't care what I go into, I don't care what it is, I've always wanted to win.

"So you couldn't say no to coach Bryant?"

I played hurt probably 40% of the time I was there at Alabama. Any time that Coach Bryant would ask, you just couldn't say no to him about anything. There was just something magical about this guy. Some of the players would go out and it would be pouring down rain. We would say we're going to have a short practice because it's getting ready to pour down rain. He would look up and the clouds would part and we would say to ourselves this guy must be some must be some kind of God or something. He was a great man. He taught all of his players. He had an impact on everybody that played and we called Coach Bryant, the old man. I carried around quotes that Coach Bryant had said and if you follow them I think they would make an impact on your life.

I was behind Johnny Davis and he was a whole lot bigger and stronger than I was at the time. He was the greatest fullback. But, I don't think Johnny ever caught a football.

"Did you see any changes in the fullback position as he tinkered with the wishbone?"

Coach Bryant tried to go to changes in the backfield. We had a fullback and a tailback and another half back on the side. That was just a power 'I' - by me playing the fullback and halfback position completely different. You got to be smart to play fullback in the wishbone because you've got to know when to clamp down on the ball. That tackle moves out and you're supposed to get the ball. By me playing both positions, I had a real good feel. I remember telling a couple of guys you missed the read.

I don't think there's a better offense that you can run if you've got the line and we had some of the greatest that ever played. None of them weighed over 250 lb. The game has changed so much now. If I ever was a coach, that's the one offense that I would implement.

What do you think the legacy of the wishbone is and how has it affected today's game?"

I think it needs to come back - if you had a coach that really knew how to coach it and had the right backs. The full-back is key to the wishbone. If you had a good fullback, I think it could work. They got this spread offense now. If you got the right quarterback and fullback that can run it would work. I don't know why they're not running it. Football is more about the fanfare and throwing the long bomb. If you go back and look under the wishbone, Alabama probably held the ball twice as much time as their opponents. In the wishbone, you grind for 5 yards and a cloud of dust. I can remember in most games we threw the ball probably 6 or 7 times. It was a big deal when we threw the ball. One of the things that Coach Bryant did was he had many multiple schemes that he used.

"What was the key for you as the fullback in making that so successful?"

Good eye coordination - first of all at fullback. If you talk to Johnny Davis he'd say the same thing. You've got to make sure that you're running the correct path. If you have to go through the guard then you have to do that because the quarterback is putting that ball in the spot. You have to run to that spot and he's not looking at you. You have to run it enough where you know that you and the quarterback are in sync. The quarterback can't be looking at you because he's doing his read. In the triple option, he had three choices. He could give to the fullback, the cornerback or run it himself. He could pitch it to the halfback coming around. We were averaging 350 or 400 yards per game and I think we led the whole time in rushing in the nation. I think it's one of the best offenses that were ever designed.

"Anything else that you would like to say?"

One of the reasons I went to Alabama was Coach Bryant had a reputation of playing a lot of guys. Coming out of high school, I really didn't think that I was good enough to play. It was an honor for me to go to Alabama and play for Coach Bryant. I never thought that I would ever be a starter, but I felt that I was good enough to play at Alabama. Had I gone to Auburn, I never would have played because they never did a whole lot of switching out. I wanted to go to Alabama because Coach Bryant would play nine backs every game. Although I might not start I would always get a chance to play. The thing about Coach Bryant was, everybody was going to play and this was why he was able to be so good every year. When a guy would graduate, the guy behind him already had lots of play. He expected you to play winning football. I remember when we were leading, Coach Bryant took the whole first-team offense out and put in the second-team. I was second team and we went out and went down the field and scored. That was how much confidence we had. Every game nobody knew who was going to start. He didn't tell so everybody had to be ready. That was one of the things that I really liked. In my sophomore year I didn't start a game, but I played more than the guy that started. Sometimes I was out there with the first-team and sometimes I was out there with the second team. It was very good for me.

"Explain the belly play"

The quarterback and the fullback have to have that feel. The full-back can't be looking at the quarterback. Anytime you would get a fumble somebody wasn't doing their job. You come out of there, you're running to a spot and that quarterback has to get it there. If that guy comes down he'll just snap the ball out. He's riding when he comes down and he's going to snap that ball out.

I'll tell you who was a good quarterback - Don Jacobs all the way. That's what made the wishbone so effective. If you've got a good quarterback, he wants to make sure that you're doing what you're supposed to be doing. We didn't have a whole lot of plays but the ones that we had, we perfected. You have to have a good offensive line and we had a great one. We had Jim Bunch, Dwight Stevenson and Buddy Aydelette. They would form a hole in the line. When the ball was snapped, they were three yards downfield before anybody touched. That's what made our offense so effective. Everybody had to be in sync. In the wishbone everybody has to do their job - even the wide receiver. If they think we're going to run, they have backs out there on the wide receiver. The cornerback would be about 5 yards away from them because they were expecting the run - I have to say 90% of the time. That's another reason I came to Alabama because I knew they were going to run the ball and there wasn't going to be a whole lot of passing. That's what made it so good. Dwight Stephenson, Jim bunch and some of those guys started the year before in my sophomore year. We had a whole new line my junior year.

I think that was one of the most exciting offenses. Today they've got a lot of pageantry - throwing the long bomb and all that stuff. The wishbone was smash mouth football. Johnny led the league in rushing my senior year. The fullback was very important in the wishbone offense. If I had it to do over again I would do the same thing.

While at Alabama Billy rushed for 1,404 yards and 7 touchdowns. In 1981 he was drafted by the Kansas City Chiefs in round 7. While there he rushed for 1,365 yards and 16 touchdowns.

Jim Bunch – Offensive Lineman – 1976-1979

"What brought you to play for Alabama under Coach Bryant?"

I'd like to say it was just destiny. When I was in high school, I had two teammates that were from Alabama and that had played football with Major Ogilvie. I was watching the Super Bowl when Namath won. When I finished high school, nobody recruited me because I was too small so I went to a prep school. We played junior varsity schools. It was just an incredible experience to be able to play at a high level, but it was a military school. It was a tough military environment that I was in. A game film went down and they just happened to see me. My first contact with Alabama was I was awakened at 2:30 in the morning and I heard that Alabama had called me. It was Coach Bryant and at the time I didn't know who Coach Bryant was because I was from Virginia. I called him and woke him up. He said somebody's playing a trick on us, so I'll have one of the coaches contact you tomorrow. Probably the biggest reason I got recruited was I had the nerve to wake up Coach Bryant. When I went to visit Alabama, Coach Bryant was not even there. He was at a book signing. When I did talk to him, he said, you probably won't play until you are a senior and I said I'm okay with that. All the schools that were recruiting me said, you don't want to go to Alabama because you won't play. So it was just a challenge.

"What was so special about the wishbone offense?"

The best thing about it is that there's no hesitation. You carry out your assignment. What I would try to do is come off the ball as fast as I could and propel my body in that direction. Whatever would come across my face I would try to block.

"You were involved in two back-to-back national championship teams which one was more memorable to you?"

They both are. It was an incredible experience. To me personally - I was hurt that year so it was a battle just to be in there. One game I wasn't supposed to play at all. The trainer said you won't play, don't even dress. So I go in the locker room right before the game and Coach Bryant came up beside me. He asked me about my general health. I said coach, I'm doing great, so he said you're going to start. That pain that was in my ankle went away but after the game I was on crutches again. It was just a battle to get in there and be a part of each game.

"What is the most memorable game that you can recall?"

We went out to play Southern Cal and they were ranked number one. I had a good game and Keith Jackson recognized me. I was at best an average player. As a typical Bear Bryant type player I have a lot of heart and really that was our offensive line. They gave it all they had, every play. Once I became a coach at Alabama, I coached one year in 1980. Just to be around that round table and listen to the stories and being a part of those coaches meetings was incredible. It was like being with King Arthur and the Knights of the Round Table. That one year was incredible.

"What was it like as Bear Bryant was perfecting the wishbone in those years?"

He was getting you to play above your natural abilities. The fans actually did not cheer a lot because they were so used to winning. Sometimes if we were ahead by a lot, they would just leave. The most memorable experience was my first game. We played against Ole Miss and we lost and I was thinking Coach Bryant was sick the last 10 years of his life. Just the sheer will of wanting to coach - he loved it. He said that if you don't throw up before each game as a coach then you don't need to coach. You need to feel that way about it as a coach just like a player.

I was fortunate that I got to play four years and each year was special. The offensive line we had in 76 was incredible, and just like 77. Probably the most unjust thing that ever happened was in 66 when they were undefeated and two-time defending national championship - they were ranked number 3. In 1950 Coach Bryant should have won a national championship at Kentucky and that would have given him nine national championships. Our most memorable player each year was Coach Bryant.

What he would say to us at practice every day was, you want to get a little bit better each day. He would cut one of our best players on the field and he would say, you're not practicing well enough and you're off the team. That player would beg to get back on the team. He would do anything he could to talk Coach Bryant into letting him back, but what he was trying to send a message to the team. It's the team first. It's all about the team, not the individual. That's why Coach Bryant was so successful. If you weren't a team player, he wouldn't care how good you were. He liked the overachievers better the great athlete. Of course we had a great number of tremendous athletes over the years, but all the guys are humble and that's what coach Bryant taught us. It's all about the team.

Jim was honored as a member of the 1979 All-America Team First Team. He played for the West Virginia Rockets in 1980.

Walter Lewis – Quarterback – 1980-1983

"How did you get recruited by Alabama?"

Coach Bryant came down and made an official visit, he challenged me and asked me some questions. One of the questions he asked me was, haven't you always dreamed of playing in that red jersey? I just told him, no I never dreamed of playing in a red jersey, my dreams were to play professional football playing for the Buffalo Bills or somebody like that. I really looked at Ohio State and USC. At the time those were the teams that were in the forefront in my eyes. One of the reasons is you had Archie Griffin at Ohio State and he was getting a lot of attention but at USC at the time they had tons and tons of black players. I wasn't looking for that it was just noticeable at the time. That's the early 70s and it was obvious Anthony Davis and all the running backs they had coming out of there and I really liked what they brought to the table. That's what I saw and I think Coach Bryant was just feeling me out. He was really behind in terms of recruiting and when I answered that, he really got a chance to see where I was so he started asking my parents questions. When he asked my mom, she said, I really don't care where he goes to school but if he came to Alabama I wouldn't want you to recruit him just to sit him on the bench so nobody else can get him. If he can play I would expect him to be able to play. That was a profound statement my mom made to Coach Bryant and Coach said if he has the ability to come in here and play, I Have no reservations in playing him. Back then the issues of black and white were prominent in that position.

Alabama only had one scholarship left so my dad said, "do you want to go to Alabama?" You need to decide what you're going to do. If you do, you need to pick up the phone and call Coach Bryant and tell him. So I picked up the phone and called Coach Bryant. They were practicing for the Sugar Bowl that year against Arkansas in 1979. Coach Bryant was in his tower, he had a phone in his tower. I told him that I wanted to come to Alabama, but what was really going through my mind was, I had turned him down and I thought is he going to have any animosity toward me? That was the extent of my recruiting with him.

"What ended up being your relationship with Coach Bryant?"

You know in today's terms he would be a rock star. He had confidants around him that would cater to him, so I didn't mix and mingle with him. Everybody was in awe of him, but I treated him with respect and he reciprocated that. One thing I appreciated about Coach Bryant was when you're in a leadership position he stands behind you and gives you what you need to be a leader. You know Coach Bryant stood in the gap and took the arrows for me for me to perform the way I did and I'm very grateful and appreciative. That's the only thing that any man can ask for in life is when you're working and trying to perform for somebody else. Coach Bryant was fair and he freed me up to do my thing and I'm very grateful for that.

"What about Joey Jones?"

I got to know him in the All-Star Game. We got to know each other. He has come a long way since then. He would challenge the system, but he is as loyal as they come, very giving in terms of football, and very supportive of me in my role. I have nothing but ultimate respect for him.

"What was unique about the passing game?"

My hat is off to Mal. He was an ultimate technician and he was all about the x's and the O's. When I watched them as a youngster in play action in the wishbone, the corners would have to commit. I never saw it until I got there where they would split the receivers out. You could dictate and balance a defense - going to their strengths or their weakness. Mal did an outstanding job doing that. They didn't know if a run was coming or a pass was coming and they were able to isolate receivers all the time. It is very difficult with a guy running at you at 4.7 and another guy running at you at 4.4, and you are running the wishbone. The corners have to read whether to come up or stay back. He's in a jam all the time. That's the dilemma that defensive backs have, and also linebackers. Because you can run a back out of the backfield in the same action. He's on a pass route and the linebackers are trying to read the run - he runs right by him. It was a mismatch for the defenders, being able to pass or run out of the wishbone.

"What are the challenges of the wishbone?"

That really wasn't a challenge and my hat's off to Richard Todd because that's who I watched as a youngster. So the aspect of the action on the wishbone came naturally to me. A couple of things that Mal taught as it relates to being able to disconnect from that fullback - that was very easy for me. The challenge in the wishbone was being able to run, but also be able to tie in the pass and to commit the timing of the receivers. Making sure you had proper footwork to run or being able to pass. Those things were a challenge initially. But once I understood my role and got a feel for what was going on defensively, it allowed me to become an effective passer utilizing the wishbone.

"How did Mal Moore coach you as the first African American to play quarterback at Alabama?"

My freshman year I didn't know how I stacked up. I wasn't there to compare myself to others I was just there to work hard and do what the coaches were telling me to do but evidently the coaches saw something different they could work with and be successful with. As a freshman I remember coming in 13th or 14th on the depth chart. When they recruited me they said we only have two or three quarterbacks. Coach Bryant would put you in a situation to see if the cream was going to rise to the top. I remember very vividly as I climbed the depth chart the coaches put enormous amounts of pressure on me. They would humiliate me in front of the team. They would grab me by the face mask and call me names. But I noticed they weren't doing that to the white players and I thought is this a racial thing? My family raised me to never really look at color as an issue, but I knew that there were issues as it relates to that. At the moment they put so much pressure on me, I remember I didn't even want to go to practice as a freshman. I didn't know what they were doing so I just kind of grinned and smiled at them when they came at me with challenges like that. What I did learn when Coach Bryant passed away and then Mal Moore was potentially going to be the coach, he actually took all the quarterbacks to dinner when he decided to go to Notre Dame. Coach Moore pulled me to the side and said, "do you remember how I used to treat you as a freshman?" I said absolutely, and he said, "let me explain to you what was going on with you being the first black quarterback here at Alabama." What Coach Bryant and I had to find out was, would you fold under us because if you would fold under us, then you would fold under the other teams. I never knew that was going on but that has paid huge dividends for me as a person. I'm talking 35 years later because that's just the way it is. In real activities there's pressure. Your character and who you are is challenged. It's just an experience that's priceless for me. I characterize that experience as The Good, The Bad and The Ugly and that was part of the ugly side, but out of the ugly comes a lot of good.

"You played in Coach Bryant's last game, the Liberty Bowl, are there any memories you want to share?"

I had never played in a game that peaks and continues. Most games have highs and lows and it goes in cycles, but that game from start to finish just kept rising in terms of the intensity and emotions. You never saw a valley. That game was so intense. I had never experienced anything like that. It generally takes me about 8 hours to wind down from a game, but that game took me about 3 days just to unwind!

During that game Coach Bryant and I got into it. It was the first time I've ever disputed anything he's ever done. I remember there was a situation where he wanted to substitute two players into a certain situation. It was third and one or fourth and one, but I didn't want those players and he called a timeout and I got in his face. He heard what I had to say and he grabbed me in my chest and he said, "Walter I'm the leader of this team and not you. If you had been doing what you're supposed to be doing in that last play we wouldn't be in this situation." The reason I didn't want to substitute those two players is that I didn't feel that in that particular situation I could really trust them. During that moment I realized I had disrespected Coach Bryant and I remember during the TV timeout I apologized to him.

Two days before he passed away I went by his office and said, I came by just to tell you that I'm sorry for disrespecting you during that game. His reaction wasn't what I thought I was going to get. He said, "Walter that's just a part of the game." He didn't say it, but what I got from him was this. I've achieved what I wanted to achieve in you. That was what he tried to do with leaders. When I got in his face he was experiencing what he wanted to get out of me as a quarterback and I was beginning to take on the reins. The reaction that I got from him is not the reaction that I thought. He thought, we made it here and me being his first black quarterback that was something he wanted to see out of any quarterback.

"To what extent do you think Alabama's wishbone era has led to the success that continues to

the present day?"

I think it was 1970 or 71 the wishbone first came on the scene. Prior to that I think there were some tough times. Which kind of led to Coach Bryant during fall practice, he just threw it in there. He made some drastic changes to adapt to what was going on collegiately in football. That kind of started the roll in the 70s in terms of the success. That kind of set the tone for Alabama football in terms of how that applies to today. The bricks, the mortar, the foundation in terms of what Nick Saban has been able to take it to a whole different level like Coach Bryant did back in the 60s and 70s. Saban has done the same thing in terms of the standard that Coach Bryant set. Coach Saban is just doing it in a different way. I really believe this in winning. It has the same formula. It's just certain ingredients that make up a winner and great coaches have it and great programs have it. Coach Bryant built the foundation, the character and what Coach Saban is doing is building on that.

"What else would you like to share about the Wishbone period?"

Well, when I first came and I started moving up the depth chart a player made a comment to me and it kind of hurt my feelings. It bothered me but in my mind I said okay, I'm putting a check mark beside this conversation and I said to myself, I'll see you down the road, Jack. Sure enough I started moving up the depth chart and Coach Bryant called me over to the first team. I got in the huddle and a couple of players had to get out of the huddle. In my mind I thought well I'll see you down the road Jack and a couple of the older players had come to me. They were sharing with me. Robbie Jones was passing on to me what the older players that were black players said. One of the things that they had adopted was that they felt they had to be twice as good as their competitors on the field because they were being watched as trailblazers. I adopted that thought process as a quarterback. I remember getting in that huddle you run the option, you pitch every play. You would pitch just to get the practice. When you pitched, that running back would run to the goal line which could be 20, 30 or 40 yards out and you jogged back. When I pitched to the running back, I said to myself, "well I'm going to run with you" and I ran to the end zone with them and jogged back. I was just doing that all the time and the other quarterbacks weren't doing that. I don't know what was going through their minds, but I remember coming back to the huddle and Major Ogilvie (remember I'm a freshman and Major is a senior). So Coach Bryant came down from the top of the tower to talk with somebody and stopped the play. During that break, Major turned to me and said "hey do you ever get tired?" I looked at him and I said "do you know who John Havelicek is?" He said, yes I do. I said, "did he ever get tired?" He said, "no he never got tired." I said "I'm just like him, I never get tired." For a freshman to say that to a senior when we're going into the Notre Dame game was something. That's the first thing that popped into my mind and I don't know how that played on Major, but you're trying to garner the support with your teammates and that couldn't have been a better answer. Major was outstanding to play with. With all the pressure that the players and the coaches were putting on me, I would lay in my bed at night and I would cry and pray. I didn't want to go back to practice, but I had the team on my shoulders and I didn't want to let them down. You got to deal with the crucible. The crucible gets all of the stuff out of you and there was some stuff coming out of me at that time growing up as a young man and a football player.

.

Coach Bryant quote – "Never quit. It is the easiest cop-out in the world. Set a goal and don't quit until you attain it. Never quit."

Coach Bryant put us in some serious situations and I remember guys crying, but he would tell us, if you quit this then you're going to quit your wife or school. If you quit it's going to make it easier to quit anything else. That's so true and that's something that was drilled in us. We used to run perfection drills. You would line up straight and come off the ball straight. These and you would run sprints as a team in 100 degree weather in two-a-days. Guys were throwing up and doing all kinds of different things. When you get in a game and things are on the line, you learn not to give in. In the wishbone everybody had to run. The lineman had to come off and run and block. Backs had to run and quarterbacks. So everybody had to run and you had to be in condition. That offense basically prepared you to be strong in those types of adversities, so I wouldn't trade my experience for anything.

"Walter, did the fan base accept you as the quarterback?"

As far as I know, I felt like 95% of the people supported me as the quarterback. I never experienced the negative side because I didn't focus on that. I didn't go looking for that. I didn't get in the papers. I felt like I knew what I was giving as a quarterback. It was everything I had and that's all that I could do. I never felt maligned by anybody. I hear stuff about guys that would do various things not block or whatever, but I never saw that on the field. People can speculate and create rumors, but I never experienced it. I wouldn't trade my experience at Alabama for anything.

In his four years at Alabama, Walter passed for 4,257 yards and 29 touchdowns. He rushed for 1,442 yards and 13 touchdowns.

He played for the Memphis Showboats of the United States Football League (USFL) and the Montreal Alouettes of the Canadian Football League. In 1984, he completed 161 passes for 1,862 yards and 15 touchdowns. He also ran 60 times for 552 yards and 5 touchdowns. In 1985, Lewis completed 97 for 1,593 yards and 16 touchdowns and also rushed 65 times for 591 yards and 4 touchdowns.

Joey Jones – Wide Receiver – 1980-1983

"Joey how did you end up at Alabama playing for Coach Bryant?"

I think that I was probably the last scholarship given. I weighed 160 pounds at that time, but I could run pretty well. Bobby Marks recruited me from Alabama, but Coach Bryant never came down there. They gave me one in 1980.

"When you finally met Coach Bryant, what was that like?"

It was like a dream come true. I walked in the dorm and he was there. He was a huge man about six foot four and a very imposing figure. I looked up at him and shook his hand and he looked down at me. He looked at coach Marks as if to say, who the heck have you brought in here to Alabama? It wasn't a real good welcome at first. I think he thought I would never play there because I was too small.

"You played near the end of the wishbone era. What was so special about the wishbone and Coach Bryant?"

Coach Bryant was obviously a great man and everybody knows he's a great coach. What I admire about him most is - he was the same guy off the field as on the field. Sitting down at dinner, he was the same man. He didn't put on a show for the cameras. He came up from tough beginnings and I always admired how he was able to be just real. I admired him so much for his honesty and integrity.

"What was so special about the way he ran the wishbone offense?"

He was a perfectionist and pushed people to their limits. We would go out to Tuscaloosa Hospital every summer and have scrimmages. I remember 40-some plays in a row and I wanted to quit. After I got done that night, I realized I can do anything. I realized what he was doing. He was pushing you over the edge. That's the kind of coach that he was. He was such a motivator of people.

"What was evolving about the wishbone in those years?"

It was really starting to fade out and people were figuring it out. Football goes in big circles. Now some people are starting to go back to the triple option stuff, but it started to fade out in those few years. It still was a great offense. I'm into coaching now and we played Navy last year. It is a very hard offense to stop. It's still one of the best offenses that has ever been.

"Was it the right scheme at that time?"

They won many national championships with it, so I think it was a pretty good offense. It always will be - anybody that has the guts to run it. It's good for recruiting because you got guys that want to throw the ball around and catch passes. It's just a great offense to run.

"What was your involvement on the field?"

Pretty much blocking. As a matter of fact if they ever called a pass play the defensive backs could always tell. That kind of gave it away. I did mainly blocking and catching long balls for touchdowns. The main thing about the wishbone is that you just run and run and all of a sudden you fake it. There's a receiver going right down the middle of the field and wide open. We had a lot of touchdowns and that was due to the wishbone offense.

"Is there one particular touchdown that sticks out in your mind?"

Probably the first one we were playing Georgia Tech. I was actually fifth string going into the season. Everybody got hurt and I had to play. My receiver coach was as nervous as he could be. He came up to me before the game and he said, don't you get me fired! I said I'll try not to get you fired. The first pass in the game I ran a 50 yard touchdown. That was a euphoric feeling as I ran into the end zone.

"What other favorite memories do you have about playing football at Alabama?"

Probably earning Coach Bryant's trust. I don't think that I had it at first in my sophomore year. I think he began to believe in me. That game when I caught my first touchdown, he put his arm around me and looked at me and smiled. He didn't say anything. He just winked at me and walked away. That meant you finally made it with me. That had a lot to do with my life - to prove to Coach Bryant that I could play. I lost my father at a young age, so he was a father figure to me and I think it propelled me the rest of my life with a confidence level that I could do anything.

"You were there in 1982, which was coach Bryant's last season what was that like?"

It was very special looking at that season and going through the last game at the Liberty Bowl. I really thought about all of the players when played for him. I thought this is all about the guys that had played for him in the last 25 years. That meant so much to him. It was just a true bond so I was just a small part of that big machine that he had created.

"Do you keep up with your former teammates and have they had a big impact on your life?"

A lot of the guys go back to the games, but I've been coaching every Saturday so I don't have an opportunity to go. I've been coaching for the last 6 years so it's very difficult to get up there. We certainly keep in touch on the phone. I'm pretty good at email now. It's a bond that you have. When I go to different cities, inevitably there is somebody that I have played with. We give each other a call and get together so it is a bond that will last the rest of my life.

"As a coach how would you grade the wishbone effectiveness?"

I would have to give it an A plus, it is the best offense that has ever been. You don't have to block anybody on that side of the football - you read them. It's a very tough physical part of the game.

Joey had 71 receptions for 1,386 yards and 15 touchdowns. He ranked third among Alabama's career touchdown receivers and seventh in career receiving yards. He was named All-SEC as a senior and chosen to participate in the Senior Bowl. He was a member of the University of Alabama's All-Decade Team for the 1980s.

He played professionally with the Birmingham Stallions of the United States Football League and the Atlanta Falcons.

Coach Gene Stallings

“Please relate that story that Darell Royal mentioned to you in the 68 Cotton Bowl”

I don't know if it's authentic or not but here's what Darell Royal told me. We were getting ready to play a game and he said the wishbone had started when he played Alabama in the Cotton Bowl. I said, I didn't know that. He put the fullback about two and a half yards behind the quarterback because Alabama's linebackers were so fast. He had the tailback back from the normal position and the fullback behind the quarterback. I don't know if that's accurate or not but that's what Darell told me. They developed the wishbone, and it was a tough offensive formation to try to defend.

“How would you describe the wishbone to someone who was not familiar with it?”

Well first of all, defensively you've got to be able to tackle the guy that they fake the ball to. It's extremely difficult to defend. You have to have three people taken care of and if you just take care of two of them the one that's left is going to get the ball, so that's the tough thing about the wishbone. Then they started moving and it started one way and going the other. That was a new dimension to it, but they didn't do that until later on; you had three people in position. One of the negatives about the wishbone was that you could put 9 or 10 people up on the line to stop the run.

“How does the wishbone affect the game today?”

I was coaching pro ball, and in pro ball we weren't involved in the wishbone. You had to stop the run on the wishbone, you had three guys that you had to defend every time. The quarterback could get the ball, the pitch man could get the ball, so that was a real problem for the defense. When they started one way and came back the other that just multiplied it.

“Do you see any evidence of the wishbone in today’s college football?”

Well it's different. Very few people now even have a quarterback up behind the center, they're back now. It's awfully hard to run a three-way option when the quarterback is not one of the option guys. In the regular wishbone, the quarterback was a runner he wasn't a passer. The halfback was running, and the fullback was running. They don't do that now because the excitement in the college games is the passing, not running the football.

“Coach, anything else you'd like to add?”

The University of Texas initiated it. Emory Bellard really developed the wishbone. It was Darell's initial idea and he was an outstanding coach. I would say that his claim to fame is that he was the “father of the wishbone”.

Coach Gene Stallings played college football at Texas A&M University where he was one of the "Junction Boys" under Coach Bryant. Later he served as the head coach at his alma mater from 1965 to 1971. Stallings was also the head coach of the Cardinals of the National Football League (1986–1989) and at the University of Alabama (1990–1996). Stallings' 1992 Alabama team completed a 13–0 season and was named the consensus national champion. His team won the inaugural SEC championship game against Florida 28-21. He was inducted into the College Football Hall of Fame as a coach on July 16, 2011.

Marc Bryant Tyson is the grandson of Coach Bryant

The first thing that pops into my mind was that my grandfather had a pool in his backyard with AstroTurf around it. As a little kid of about 10, I remember they put in this huge balloon that filled up the entire pool that said 200th win.

"Do you remember anything about the game itself?"

I remember the sugar bowls and especially Major Ogilvie running down the sideline with Joey Jones blocking for him. Those were two of my grandmother's favorites; I called her grandmom and I called him "Papa". I just remember Major going down there, moving his shoulder pads and scoring there in the Sugar Bowl. It was just outstanding.

"Do you remember asking him why he went to the wishbone?"

As a kid he didn't necessarily give me any insight, but I've heard so much just growing up. He was going to figure something out, develop some niche so his players could compete with the level of talent around the country.

My son Paul is a pro style quarterback. But Papa would have changed only if it would have helped the team. He would have sat my son on the bench if he thought the wishbone was a better offense.

You've got to remember "the junction boys", but the wishbone era was very special. I love that you are doing this project on them because it's a special group of guys. The guys in the wishbone have a bond. It's a different version of the junction boys and they now have their own name.

Quarterback Terry Davis

Terry Davis and Coach Bryant

Coach Bryant and Terry Davis 1971 Iron Bowl

Terry Davis and Steve Bisceglia -1972

Johnny Musso and Terry Davis

Johnny Musso

Coach Bryant and Johnny Musso Working It Out

Joe LaBue

Jimmy Jones, engineer; Doug Layton, color
John Forney, play-by-play; Bert Bank
producer.

Radio Voice of the TIDE

Italian Backfield 1971 LaBue, Bisceglia, Musso

Before she was an actress, author and producer, Sela Ward was a University of Alabama cheerleader, Chi O sorority and homecoming queen. Sela attended Alabama at the heart of the wishbone era.

Wilbur Jackson

Wishbone Formation

Ellis Beck

John Hannah

Jim Kraph

Steve Sprayberry

Wayne Wheeler

Rutledge Brothers and Tim Card at Paul W. Bryant Museum

Quarterback Gary Rutledge

Quarterback Jeff Rutledge

Coach Mal Moore and Jeff Rutledge 1978 Sugar Bowl

Quarterback Richard Todd

Johnny Davis

All American Fullback Johnny Davis and Tim Card at Jimmy Rane Golf Tournament

Ozzie Newsome

Tony Nathan

Coach Bryant and Major Ogilvie

Dwight Stephenson

Quarterback Steadman Shealy

Billy Jackson

Jim Bunch

Quarterback Walter Lewis

Joey Jones

Coach Bryant and Offensive Coordinator Mal Moore Strategizing

Coach Bryant with Friend Keith Jackson

Coach Bryant carried to the locker room –

1973 Tennessee Victory

Paul “Bear” Bryant (1913-1983)

He grew up with eight siblings on a farm in Arkansas with a widowed mother. The legend is that at thirteen, he wrestled a bear at a carnival for a dollar. While in the Navy in World War II, he saved the lives of many of his fellow sailors when their ship was struck. At 6’3” with a distinctive voice, he was a imposing figure who dominated a room with his mere presence.

In all his years of coaching, he only had one losing season, his first at Texas A&M. This was the famous season when he took the team for a summer camp in Junction where many of the players quit as it was so tough. Within a few seasons, the team was undefeated and Bryant went on to coach at Alabama from 1958 – 1982. He won six national championships and thirteen SEC championships, compiling a lifetime record of 323-85-17.

Bryant passed away on January 26, 1983 at age 69, only four weeks after retiring. On his hand at the time of his death was the only piece of jewelry he ever wore, a gold ring inscribed "Junction Boys". A month after his death, Bryant was posthumously awarded the Presidential Medal of Freedom, the nation's highest civilian award, by President Ronald Reagan.

Bryant kept a poem by Wilson Heartsill in his wallet his whole life and would often read it to his players. It spoke to his life philosophy and what he wished to impart to his teams, beyond football.

"This is the beginning of a new day. God has given me this day to use as I will. I can waste it or use it for good.

What I do today is very important because I am exchanging a day of my life for it. When tomorrow comes, this day will be gone forever, leaving something in its place I have traded for it. I want it to be a gain, not a loss – good not evil. Success, not failure, in order that I shall not regret the price I paid for it."

Two Gentlemen – Paul Bryant and Joe Paterno

The relationship between Bear Bryant and Joe Paterno was very special. They shared much of the same philosophy about football and life. They believed that football was a learning experience meant to prepare one for success in the future. They were gentlemen who loved competing against each other, but remained friends who had the upmost respect for one another. They believed that their players were students first and athletes second and did not hesitate to punish those who did not perform in the classroom as well as on the field. Of course neither would tolerate any misbehavior off the field.

When Joe Paterno was hired at Penn State as head coach, there was no formal contract. Five years later when Coach Bryant heard this, he was angered. He said to Paterno, "You get yourself a contract and be sure that you get them to include two hundred tickets. Two hundred tickets will get you a lot of favors".

Paterno once said of Bryant, "He had this – I don't know what you call it, but I guess it was charisma, it was really bigger than charisma. It's the thing that great generals have. Patton had it. MacArthur had it. He would say, 'Do something,' and people would do it. Why? They were afraid of him. They loved him. They wanted to please him. He just had that thing leaders have."

When they played in Happy Valley in 1981, Bryant called Paterno.

Bryant: Joe, you know the governor, don't you?

Paterno: Yeah, I know him a little.

Bryant: Good. We gotta land our plane up in Harrisburg. If you could, call up the governor and get him to close off the roads and get us a police escort up there after the game, I'd be appreciative."

Although the governor refused when he called, Paterno observed, "But you know what? You better believe Bear Bryant would have gotten us a police escort in Alabama. That's the difference. The only people who listen to me are the ones who have to listen or else I'll bench them. Everybody listened to Bear Bryant."

Once Paterno said, "Bear Bryant was the best coach. John McKay used to say, 'Bear's not *a* coach, he's *the* coach. I wanted to beat *the* coach." Paterno never beat Bear Bryant's teams in the four times they competed.

Bryant is quoted as saying, "I'm delighted to be playing Penn State, a great educational institution with a great deep-rooted football tradition and the leading coach in America. " Paterno responded, "I don't want to argue with him, (about being 'the leading coach').

.

Appendix

Memorable Quotes by Coach Paul "Bear" Bryant

"It's not the will to win that matters-everyone has that. It's the will to prepare to win that matters."

"I'm no miracle man. I guarantee nothing but hard work."

"I know what it takes to win. If I can sell them on what it takes to win, then we are not going to lose too many football games."

"Losing doesn't make me want to quit. It makes me want to fight that much harder."

"It's not the will to win that matters – everyone has that. It's the will to prepare to win that matters."

"Never quit. It is the easiest cop-out in the world. Set a goal and don't quit until you attain it. When you do attain it, set another goal, and don't quit until you reach it. Never quit."

"There's a lot of blood, sweat, and guts between dreams and success."

"If anything goes bad, I did it. If anything goes semi-good, we did it. If anything goes really good, then you did it. That's all it takes to get people to win football games for you."

"I think the most important thing of all for any team is a winning attitude. The coaches must have it. The players must have it. The student body must have it. If you have dedicated players who believe in themselves, you don't need a lot of talent."

"If a man is a quitter, I'd rather find out in practice than in a game. I ask for all a player has so I'll know later what I can expect."

"The idea of molding men means a lot to me."

"You must learn how to hold a team together. You must lift some men up, calm others down, until finally they've got one heartbeat. Then you've got yourself a team."

"If wanting to win is a fault, as some of my critics seem to insist, then I plead guilty. I like to win. I know no other way. It's in my blood."

"If you believe in yourself and have dedication and pride – and never quit – you'll be a winner. The price of victory is high but so are the rewards."

"Get the winners into the game."

"Set goals – high goals for you and your organization. When your organization has a goal to shoot for, you create teamwork, people working for a common good."

"The old lessons (work, self-discipline, sacrifice, teamwork, fighting to achieve) aren't being taught by many people other than football coaches these days. The football coach has a captive audience and can teach these lessons because the communication lines between himself and his players are more wide open than between kids and parents. We better teach these lessons or else the country's future population will be made up of a majority of crooks, drug addicts, or people on relief."

"Sacrifice. Work. Self-discipline. I teach these things, and my boys don't forget them when they leave."

"I'll never give up on a player regardless of his ability as long as he never gives up on himself. In time he will develop."

"Don't give up at halftime. Concentrate on winning the second half."

"Don't talk too much. Don't pop off. Don't talk after the game until you cool off."

"Mama wanted me to be a preacher. I told her coachin' and preachin' were a lot alike."

"It's awfully important to win with humility. It's also important to lose. I hate to lose worse than anyone, but if you never lose you won't know how to act. If you lose with humility, then you can come back."

"In life, you'll have your back up against the wall many times. You might as well get used to it."

"The biggest mistake coaches make is taking borderline cases and trying to save them. I'm not talking about grades now, I'm talking about character. I want to know before a boy enrolls about his home life, and what his parents want him to be."

"There is no sin in not liking to play; it's a mistake for a boy to be there if he doesn't want to."

"In a crisis, don't hide behind anything or anybody. They're going to find you anyway."

"Be aware of "yes" men. Generally, they are losers. Surround yourself with winners. Never forget – people win."

"If there is one thing that has helped me as a coach, it's my ability to recognize winners, or good people who can become winners by paying the price."

"You take those little rascals, talk to them good, pat them on the back, let them think they are good, and they will go out and beat the biguns."

"If you whoop and holler all the time, the players just get used to it."

"If you want to coach you have three rules to follow to win. One, surround yourself with people who can't live without football. I've had a lot of them. Two, be able to recognize winners. They come in all forms. And, three, have a plan for everything. A plan for practice, a plan for the game. A plan for being ahead, and a plan for being behind 20-0 at half, with your quarterback hurt and the phones dead, with it raining cats and dogs and no rain gear because the equipment man left it at home."

"My approach to the game has been the same at all the places I've been. Vanilla. The sure way. That means, first of all, to win physically. If you got eleven on a field, and they beat the other eleven physically, they'll win. They will start forcing mistakes. They'll win in the fourth quarter."

"Little things make the difference. Everyone is well prepared in the big things, but only the winners perfect the little things."

"The first time you quit, it's hard. The second time, it gets easier. The third time, you don't even have to think about it."

"But there's one thing about quitters you have to guard against – they are contagious. If one boy goes, the chances are he'll take somebody with him, and you don't want that. So when they would start acting that way, I used to pack them up and get them out, or embarrass them, or do something to turn them around."

"Scout yourself. Have a buddy who coaches scout you."

"People who are in it for their own good are individualists. They don't share the same heartbeat that makes a team so great. A great unit, whether it be football or any organization, shares the same heartbeat."

"I told them my system was based on the "ant plan," that I'd gotten the idea watching a colony of ants in Africa during the war. A whole bunch of ants working toward a common goal."

"We can't have two standards, one set for the dedicated young men who want to do something ambitious and one set for those who don't."

"When you make a mistake, there are only three things you should ever do about it: 1. Admit it. 2. Learn from it, and 3. Don't repeat it."

"I honestly believe that if you are willing to out-condition the opponent, have confidence in your ability, be more aggressive than your opponent and have a genuine desire for team victory, you will become the national champions. If you have all the above, you will acquire confidence and poise, and you will have those intangibles that win the close ones."

"Don't ever give up on ability. Don't give up on a player who has it."

"A good, quick, small team can beat a big, slow team any time."

"I have always tried to teach my players to be fighters. When I say that, I don't mean put up your dukes and get in a fistfight over something. I'm talking about facing adversity in your life. There is not a person alive who isn't going to have some awfully bad days in their lives. I tell my players that what I mean by fighting is when your house burns down, and your wife runs off with the drummer, and you've lost your job and all the odds are against you. What are you going to do? Most people just lay down and quit. Well, I want my people to fight back."

"I always want my players to show class, knock'em down, pat on the back, and run back to the huddle."

"I tell young players who want to be coaches, who think they can put up with all the headaches and heartaches, can you live without it? If you can live without it, don't get in it."

"If they don't have a winning attitude, I don't want them."

"I have tried to teach them to show class, to have pride, and to display character. I think football, winning games, takes care of itself if you do that."

"What are you doing here? Tell me why you are here. If you are not here to win a national championship, you're in the wrong place. You boys are special. I don't want my players to be like other students. I want special people. You can learn a lot on the football field that isn't taught in the home, the church, or the classroom. There are going to be days when you think you've got no more to give and then you're going to give plenty more. You are going to have pride and class. You are going to be very special. You are going to win the national championship for Alabama."

"If you want to walk the heavenly streets of gold, you gotta know the password, "Roll, Tide, Roll!"

"Losing doesn't make me want to quit. It makes me want to fight that much harder."

"It's not the will to win that matters – everyone has that. It's the will to prepare to win that matters."

"Never quit. It is the easiest cop-out in the world. Set a goal and don't quit until you attain it. When you do attain it, set another goal, and don't quit until you reach it. Never quit."

"There's a lot of blood, sweat, and guts between dreams and success."

"If anything goes bad, I did it. If anything goes semi-good, we did it. If anything goes really good, then you did it. That's all it takes to get people to win football games for you."

"I think the most important thing of all for any team is a winning attitude. The coaches must have it. The players must have it. The student body must have it. If you have dedicated players who believe in themselves, you don't need a lot of talent."

"If a man is a quitter, I'd rather find out in practice than in a game. I ask for all a player has so I'll know later what I can expect."

"The idea of molding men means a lot to me."

"You must learn how to hold a team together. You must lift some men up, calm others down, until finally they've got one heartbeat. Then you've got yourself a team."

"If wanting to win is a fault, as some of my critics seem to insist, then I plead guilty. I like to win. I know no other way. It's in my blood."

"If you believe in yourself and have dedication and pride – and never quit – you'll be a winner. The price of victory is high but so are the rewards."

"Get the winners into the game."

"Set goals – high goals for you and your organization. When your organization has a goal to shoot for, you create teamwork, people working for a common good."

"The old lessons (work, self-discipline, sacrifice, teamwork, fighting to achieve) aren't being taught by many people other than football coaches these days. The football coach has a captive audience and can teach these lessons because the communication lines between himself and his players are more wide open than between kids and parents. We better teach these lessons or else the country's future population will be made up of a majority of crooks, drug addicts, or people on relief."

"Sacrifice. Work. Self-discipline. I teach these things, and my boys don't forget them when they leave."

"I'll never give up on a player regardless of his ability as long as he never gives up on himself. In time he will develop."

"Don't give up at halftime. Concentrate on winning the second half."

"Don't talk too much. Don't pop off. Don't talk after the game until you cool off."

"Mama wanted me to be a preacher. I told her coachin' and preachin' were a lot alike."

"It's awfully important to win with humility. It's also important to lose. I hate to lose worse than anyone, but if you never lose you won't know how to act. If you lose with humility, then you can come back."

"In life, you'll have your back up against the wall many times. You might as well get used to it."

"The biggest mistake coaches make is taking borderline cases and trying to save them. I'm not talking about grades now, I'm talking about character. I want to know before a boy enrolls about his home life, and what his parents want him to be."

"There is no sin in not liking to play; it's a mistake for a boy to be there if he doesn't want to."

"In a crisis, don't hide behind anything or anybody. They're going to find you anyway."

"Be aware of "yes" men. Generally, they are losers. Surround yourself with winners. Never forget – people win."

"If there is one thing that has helped me as a coach, it's my ability to recognize winners, or good people who can become winners by paying the price."

"You take those little rascals, talk to them good, pat them on the back, let them think they are good, and they will go out and beat the biguns."

"If you whoop and holler all the time, the players just get used to it."

"If you want to coach you have three rules to follow to win. One, surround yourself with people who can't live without football. I've had a lot of them. Two, be able to recognize winners. They come in all forms. And, three, have a plan for everything. A plan for practice, a plan for the game. A plan for being ahead, and a plan for being behind 20-0 at half, with your quarterback hurt and the phones dead, with it raining cats and dogs and no rain gear because the equipment man left it at home."

"My approach to the game has been the same at all the places I've been. Vanilla. The sure way. That means, first of all, to win physically. If you got eleven on a field, and they beat the other eleven physically, they'll win. They will start forcing mistakes. They'll win in the fourth quarter."

"Little things make the difference. Everyone is well prepared in the big things, but only the winners perfect the little things."

"The first time you quit, it's hard. The second time, it gets easier. The third time, you don't even have to think about it."

"But there's one thing about quitters you have to guard against – they are contagious. If one boy goes, the chances are he'll take somebody with him, and you don't want that. So when they would start acting that way, I used to pack them up and get them out, or embarrass them, or do something to turn them around."

"Scout yourself. Have a buddy who coaches scout you."

"I'm no miracle man. I guarantee nothing but hard work."

"I know what it takes to win. If I can sell them on what it takes to win, then we are not going to lose too many football games."

"People who are in it for their own good are individualists. They don't share the same heartbeat that makes a team so great. A great unit, whether it be football or any organization, shares the same heartbeat."

"I told them my system was based on the "ant plan," that I'd gotten the idea watching a colony of ants in Africa during the war. A whole bunch of ants working toward a common goal."

"We can't have two standards, one set for the dedicated young men who want to do something ambitious and one set for those who don't."

"When you make a mistake, there are only three things you should ever do about it: 1. Admit it. 2. Learn from it, and 3. Don't repeat it."

"I honestly believe that if you are willing to out-condition the opponent, have confidence in your ability, be more aggressive than your opponent and have a genuine desire for team victory, you will become the national champions. If you have all the above, you will acquire confidence and poise, and you will have those intangibles that win the close ones."

"Don't ever give up on ability. Don't give up on a player who has it."

"A good, quick, small team can beat a big, slow team any time."

"I have always tried to teach my players to be fighters. When I say that, I don't mean put up your dukes and get in a fistfight over something. I'm talking about facing adversity in your life. There is not a person alive who isn't going to have some awfully bad days in their lives. I tell my players that what I mean by fighting is when your house burns down, and your wife runs off with the drummer, and you've lost your job and all the odds are against you. What are you going to do? Most people just lay down and quit. Well, I want my people to fight back."

"I always want my players to show class, knock'em down, pat on the back, and run back to the huddle."

"I tell young players who want to be coaches, who think they can put up with all the headaches and heartaches, can you live without it? If you can live without it, don't get in it."

"If they don't have a winning attitude, I don't want them."

"I have tried to teach them to show class, to have pride, and to display character. I think football, winning games, takes care of itself if you do that."

"What are you doing here? Tell me why you are here. If you are not here to win a national championship, you're in the wrong place. You boys are special. I don't want my players to be like other students. I want special people. You can learn a lot on the football field that isn't taught in the home, the church, or the classroom. There are going to be days when you think you've got no more to give and then you're going to give plenty more. You are going to have pride and class. You are going to be very special. You are going to win the national championship for Alabama."

"If you want to walk the heavenly streets of gold, you gotta know the password, "Roll, Tide, Roll!"

Alabama Scores – 1971 1982

1971 – Won 11, Lost 1 SEC Champions

Southern Cal 17-10

Southern Miss 42-6

Florida 38-0

Mississippi 48-6

Vanderbilt 48-0

Tennessee 42-15

Houston 34-20

LSU 14-7

Miami 31-3

Auburn 31-7

Nebraska 6-38 Orange Bowl

1972 Won 10, Lost 2 SEC Champions

Duke 35-12

Kentucky 35-0

Vanderbilt 48-21

Georgia 25-7

Florida 24-7

Tennessee 17-10

Southern Miss 48-11

Miss. State 58-14

LSU 35-21

Virginia Tech. 52-13

Auburn 16-17

Texas 13-17 Cotton

1973 Won 11, Lost 1 UPI National Champions SEC Champions

California 66-0

Kentucky 28-14

Vanderbilt 44-0

Georgia 28-14

Florida 35-14

Tennessee 42-21

Virginia Tech. 77-6

Miss. State 35-0

Miami 42-13

LSU 21-7

Auburn 35-0

Notre Dame 23-24 Sugar Bowl

1974 Won 11, Lost 1 SEC Champions

Maryland 21-16

Southern Miss. 52-0

Vanderbilt 23-10

Mississippi 35-21

Florida State 8-7

Tennessee 28-6

TCU 41-3

Miss. State 35-0

LSU 30-0

Miami 28-7

Auburn 17-13

Notre Dame 11-13 Orange Bowl

1975 Won 11, Lost 1 SEC Champions

Missouri 7-20

Clemson 56-0

Vanderbilt 40-7

Mississippi 32-6

Washington 52-0

Tennessee 30-7

TCU 45-0

Miss. State 21-10

LSU 23-10

Southern Miss. 27-6

Auburn 28-0

Penn. State 13-6 Sugar Bowl

1976 Won 9, Lost 3

Mississippi 7-10

SMU 56-3

Vanderbilt 42-14

Georgia 0-21

Southern Miss. 24-8

Tennessee 20-13

Louisville 24-3

Miss. State 34-17

LSU 28-17

Notre Dame 18-21

Auburn 38-7

UCLA 36-6 Liberty Bowl

1977 Won 11, Lost 1 SEC Champions

Mississippi 34-13

Nebraska 24-31

Vanderbilt 24-12

Georgia 18-10

Southern Cal. 21-20

Tennessee 24-10

Louisville 55-6

Miss. State 37-7

LSU 24-3

Miami 36-0

Auburn 48-21

Ohio State 35-6 Sugar Bowl

1978 Won 11, Lost 1 AP National Champions SEC Champions

Nebraska 20-3

Missouri 38-20

Southern Cal. 14-24

Vanderbilt 51-28

Washington 20-17

Florida 23-12

Tennessee 30-17

Virginia Tech. 35-0

Miss. State 35-14

LSU 31-10

Auburn 34-16

Penn. State 14-7 Sugar Bowl

1979 Won 12, Lost 0 AP/UPI National Champions SEC Champions

Georgia Tech. 30-6

Baylor 45-0

Vanderbilt 66-3

Wichita State 38-0

Florida 40-0

Tennessee 27-17

Virginia Tech. 31-7

Miss. State 24-7

LSU 3-0

Miami 30-0

Auburn 25-18

Arkansas 24-9

1980 Won 10, Lost 2

Georgia Tech. 26-3

Mississippi 59-35

Vanderbilt 41-0

Kentucky 45-0

Rutgers 17-13

Tennessee 27-0

Southern Miss. 42-7

Miss. State 3-6

LSU 28-7

Notre Dame 0-7

Auburn 34-18

Baylor 30-2 Cotton Bowl

1981 Won 9, Lost 2, Tied 1 SEC Champions

LSU 24-7

Georgia Tech. 21-24

Kentucky 19-10

Vanderbilt 28-7

Mississippi 38-7

Southern Miss. 13-3

Tennessee 38-19

Rutgers 31-7

Miss. State 13-10

Penn. State 31-16

Auburn 28-17

Texas 12-14 Cotton Bowl

1982 Won 8, Lost 4

Georgia Tech. 45-7

Mississippi 42-14

Vanderbilt 24-21

Arkansas State 34-7

Penn. State 42-21

Tennessee 28-35

Cincinnati 21-3

Miss. State 20-12

LSU 10-20

Southern Miss. 29-38

Auburn 22-23

Illinois 21-15 Liberty Bowl

Alabama Records in the wishbone Era

- yards gained per game (480.7 in 1973)
- rushing attempts in a season (763 in 1979)
- rushing yards gained in a season (4,027 in 1973)
- rushing yards per game for a season (366.1 in 1973)
- yards per rush for a season (6.06 in 1973)
- rushing touchdowns (43 in 1973)

1971 Roster

1971 Alabama Crimson Tide football team roster						
Players						Coaches
Offense				Defense		
Pos.	#	Name	Class	Name	Class	
WR	84	David Bailey	Sr	Wayne Atkinson	Jr	
OG	53	Marvin Barron	Jr	Jeff Beard	Sr	
				Jeff Blitz	Jr	
RB	35	Ellis Beck	Jr	Robin Cary	So	
RB	44	Steve Bisceglia	Jr	Andy Cross	Jr	
OT	65	Buddy Brown	So	John Croyle	Jr	
TE	43	Richard Bryan	So	Jimmy Dawson	So	
				Joe Doughty	So	
C	59	Chip Burke	So	Woody Flowers	So	
WR	46	Jerry Cash	Sr	Don Groves	So	
OG		Joe Cochran	So	Wayne Hall	Jr	
OT	70	Don Cokely	Sr	teve Higginbotham	Sr	
TE	47	Wayne Cotton	Jr	Ed Hines	Sr	
OT	75	Allen Cox	Jr	Skip Kubelius	So	
QB	10	Terry Davis	Jr	Jim Krapf	Jr	
RB	39	Steve Dean	Jr	Frank Lary	So	

Pos	No.	Name	Class
OT	91	Mike Denson	So
WR	31	Warren Dyar	Jr
C	69	Mike Eckenrod	Jr
OG	62	Tommy Ford	Jr
C	55	Jimmy Grammer	Sr
OT	73	John Hannah	Jr
QB	17	Butch Hobson	Jr
TE	86	Jimmy Horton	Jr
OG	60	Morris Hunt	Jr
WR	80	Wilbur Jackson	So
WR	19	Pat Keever	So
RB	30	Joe LaBue	Jr
C	58	Rand Lambert	So
C	51	Fred Marshall	Sr
TE	87	Randy Moore	Jr
RB	20	Phil Murphy	So
RB	22	Johnny Musso	Sr
WR	6	Pete Pappas	So

Name	Class
Tom Lusk	Jr
Greg Mantooth	So
Bob McKinney	Jr
David McMakin	So
Noah Miller	So
John Mitchell	Jr
Lanny Norris	Jr
Robin Parkhouse	Sr
Jim Patterson	Sr
Max Raines	So
Mike Riley	Fr
Ronnie Robertson	So
Steve Root	Sr
Jeff Rouzie	Jr
Robby Rowan	Jr
Terry Rowell	Sr
Johnny Sharpless	So
Chuck Strickland	So
Tom Surlas	Sr
Carl Tayloe	Jr
Steve Wade	Jr
David Watkins	So

OG	71	Steve Patterson	So
C	53	Pat Raines	Jr
OG	79	Gary Reynolds	So
RB	16	Ron Richardson	Sr
QB	15	Benny Rippetoe	Sr
OG	61	John Rogers	So
OG	68	Rick Rogers	So
OT	72	Jimmy Rosser	Sr
QB	11	Gary Rutledge	So
WR	27	Bubba Sawyer	Sr
QB	14	Billy Sexton	Jr
TE	85	Jim Simmons	Sr
RB	24	Paul Spivey	So
OT	78	Steve Sprayberry	So
WR	34	Tommy Steakley	Sr
WR	88	Danny Taylor	Jr
WR	82	Wayne Wheeler	Jr

Mitchell Weaver	Jr
Steve Williams	Sr

OG	66	Jack White	Sr
WR	92	Dexter Wood	Jr
TE	7	Glenn Woodruff	Sr

Start Game with Inside vs 75   FF version 70-6-1
TAKE good splits

38/9 = cut splits down
one loop vs 75
go inside vs
everything else

38/9 Seal –

Ct 18/19 Block #2

Seal – Tackle Seal
only when #2
in LBer

Purple – None except
on Ct 18/19 vs 6-5

TRAP – Gd know if
tight END is there

o

Wishbone Play Notes Attributed to Coach Mal Moore

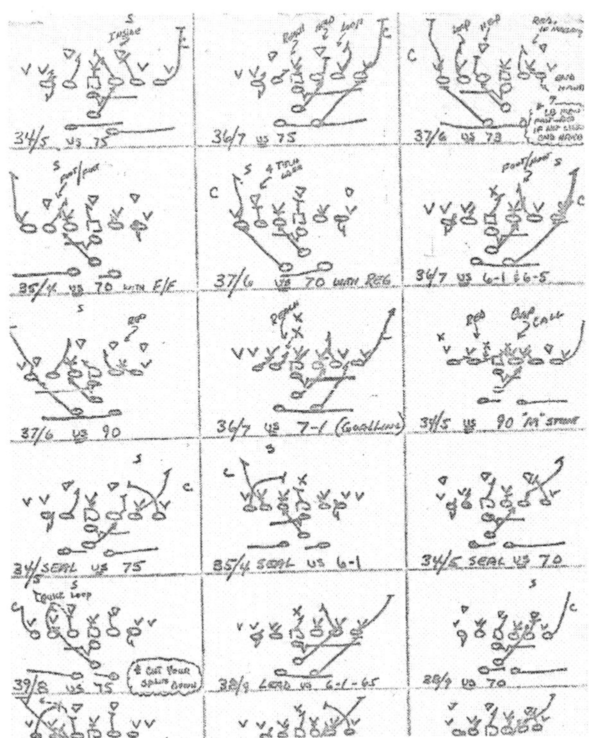
34/5 vs 75
36/7 vs 75
35/4 vs 70 with F/F
37/6 vs 70 with REG
34/7 vs 6-1 & 6-5
37/6 vs 90
36/7 vs 7-1 (Goalline)
34/5 vs 90 "M" stunt
34/SEAL vs 75
35/4 SEAL vs 6-1
34/5 SEAL vs 70

Ct 10/11 vs 75	*Ct 10/11 BLOCK REG VERSUS ANY OTHER FRONT!	30/31 vs 75
31/30 vs 6-1	30/31 CAN USE FOLD if NEEDED	Ct 40/21 vs 75
Ct 21/40 vs 6-1	* TIGHT END 22/43 TRAP vs 75	* NO TIGHT END 43/22 TRAP vs 75
Pass 34/5 vs 75	Pass 37/6 vs 6-1 or 6-5	Pass 36/7 vs 70
75 P37/5 - P36/4 Bootleg	P35/4 Bootleg vs 70	P36/4 Bootleg
ALL PASSES BLOCKED ALIKE [illegible]	*REMEMBER COACHING POINTS ON REVERSE [illegible]	

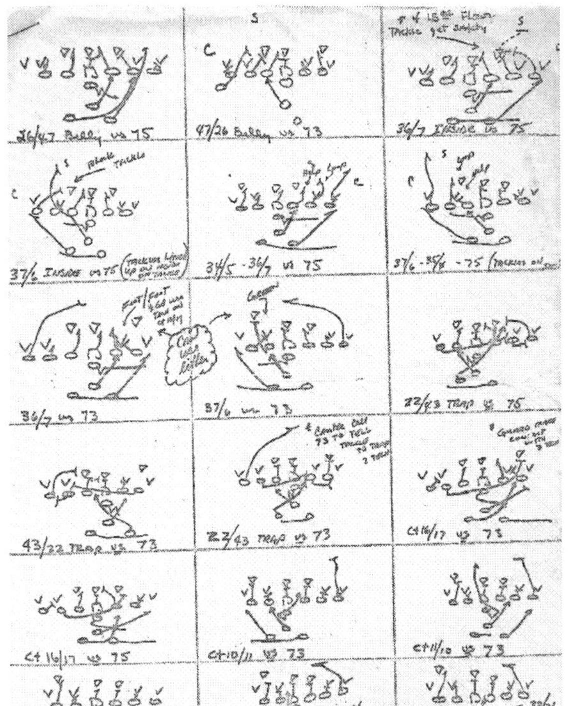

Wishbone Plays Courtesy Coach Jimmy Sharpe

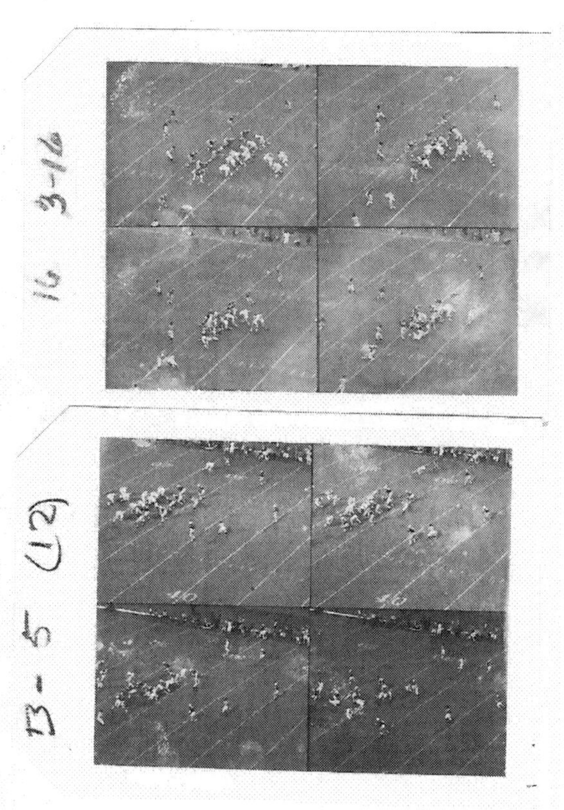
16 3-16
B-5 (12)

Polaroid Photos from the press box of Wishbone Plays courtesy of Coach Jimmy Sharpe

Shorty Price

For decades, William Ralph Price - known to one and all as "Shorty" due to his five foot stature - was perhaps the Alabama Crimson Tide football team's most famous, fan.

A student during the high point of Frank Thomas' powerful 1940s Crimson Tide teams, Price's lifelong devotion to Alabama football began when he was elected to the cheerleading squad.

Over the next several decades, he became a staple at Alabama games; dressing in garish outfits, smoking his trademark Tampa Nugget cigars and standing on the in-field wall exhorting the crowd to cheer with him. Price was as likely to be found dancing in the aisles as climbing the goalposts.

Price died in an automobile accident near Montgomery on Nov. 1, 1980 on the way to attend the Alabama vs. Mississippi State game in Jackson, Miss.

Teams using the wishbone

- 1968 Texas Longhorns [9-1-1]
- 1969 Texas Longhorns [11-0] AP and UPI national champions
- 1970 Texas Longhorns [11-1] UPI national champions
- **1971 Alabama Crimson Tide [11-1]**
- 1971 Oklahoma Sooners [11-1] 4 players ran for over 625 yards
- 1971 Texas Longhorns [8-3]
- **1972 Alabama Crimon Tide [10-2]**
- 1972 Oklahoma Sooners [11-1] 8 players ran for over 240 yards
- 1972 Purdue Boilermakers [6-5] Ran for 2,592 Yards
- 1972 Texas Longhorns [10-1]
- 1972 UCLA Bruins [8-3]
- **1973 Alabama Crimson Tide [11-1] UPI national champions**
- 1973 Oklahoma Sooners [10-0-1] 3 players ran for over 880 yards
- 1973 Purdue Boilermakes [5-6] Ran for 2,124 Yards
- 1973 Texas Longhorns [8-3]
- 1973 UCLA Bruins [9-2]
- 1974 Army Black Knights [3-8]
- 1974 Florida Gators [8-4] 4 players ran for over 398 yards
- 1974 Oklahoma Sooners [11-0] AP national champions; 6 players ran for over 375 yards
- 1974 Texas Longhorns [8-4]
- 1974 Texas A&M Aggies [8-3]
- 1975 Florida Gators [9-3] 5 players ran for over 244 yards
- 1975 Oklahoma Sooners [11-1] AP and UPI national champions; 6 players ran for over 322 yards
- 1975 Texas Longhorns [10-2]
- 1975 Texas A&M Aggies [10-2]
- 1976 Florida Gators [8-4] 6 players ran for over 233 yards

- 1976 Holy Cross Crusaders [3-8]
- 1976 Kentucky Wildcats [8-4] 4 players ran for over 504 yards
- 1976 Oklahoma Sooners [9-2-1] 5 players ran for over 443 yards
- 1976 Texas A&M Aggies [10-2]
- 1977 Florida Gators [6-4-1] 4 players ran for over 353 yards
- 1977 Holy Cross Crusaders [2-9]
- 1977 Kentucky Wildcats [10-1] 5 players ran for over 338 yards
- 1977 Oklahoma Sooners [10-2] 5 players ran for over 354 yards
- 1977 Pennsylvania Quakers [5-4]
- 1978 Oklahoma Sooners [11-1] 4 players ran for over 408 yards
- 1979 Kentucky Wildcats [5-6] 3 players ran for over 460 yards
- 1979 Mississippi State Bulldogs [3-8] 4 players ran for over 378 yards
- 1979 Oklahoma Sooners [11-1] 4 players ran for over 358 yards
- 1980 Mississippi State Bulldogs [9-3] 4 players ran for over 438 yards
- 1980 Oklahoma Sooners [10-2] 7 players ran for over 292 yards
- 1981 Air Force Falcons [4-7] 5 players ran for over 235 yards
- 1981 Auburn Tigers [5-6] 3 players ran for over 442 yards
- 1981 Mississippi State Bulldogs [8-4] 4 players ran for over 258 yards
- 1981 Oklahoma Sooners [7-4-1] 3 players ran for over 442 yards
- 1982 Air Force Falcons [8-5] 5 players ran for over 404 yards
- 1982 Auburn Tigers [9-3] 4 players ran for over 284 yards
- 1982 Mississippi State Bulldogs [5-6] 5 players ran for over 349 yards
- 1982 Oklahoma Sooners [8-4] 4 players ran for over 621 yards
- 1983 Air Force Falcons [10-2] 3 players ran for over 767 yards
- 1983 Auburn Tigers [11-1] 3 players ran for over 604 yards
- 1983 Mississippi State Bulldogs [3-8] 6 players ran for over 232 yards
- 1983 Oklahoma Sooners [8-4] 4 players ran for over 369 yards
- 1984 Air Force Falcons [8-4] 6 players ran for over 232 yards

- 1984 Army Black Knights [8-3-1]
- 1984 Auburn Tigers [9-4] 5 players ran for over 299 yards
- 1984 Mississippi State Bulldogs [4-7] 6 players ran for over 234 yards
- 1984 Oklahoma Sooners [9-2-1] 4 players ran for over 465 yards
- 1985 Air Force Falcons [12-1] 4 players ran for over 492 yards
- 1985 Army Black Knights [9-3]
- 1985 Colorado Buffaloes [7-5] 5 players ran for over 269 yards
- 1985 Oklahoma Sooners [11-1] 7 players ran for over 240 yards
- 1986 Air Force Falcons [6-5] 4 players ran for over 275 yards
- 1986 Army Black Knights [6-5]
- 1986 Colorado Buffaloes [6-6] 4 players ran for over 224 yards
- 1986 Oklahoma Sooners [11-1] 9 players ran for over 283 yards
- 1987 Air Force Falcons [9-4] 6 players ran for over 384 yards
- 1987 Army Black Knights [5-6]
- 1987 Colorado Buffaloes [7-4] 6 players ran for over 332 yards
- 1987 Michigan Wolverines [8-4]
- 1987 Missouri Tigers [5-6] 3 players ran for over 552 yards
- 1987 Navy Midshipmen [2-9]
- 1987 Nebraska Cornhuskers [10-2]
- 1987 Oklahoma Sooners [11-1] 6 players ran for over 683 yards
- 1988 Air Force Falcons [5-7] 5 players ran for over 576 yards
- 1988 Army Black Knights [9-3]
- 1988 Colorado Buffaloes [8-4] 5 players ran for over 257 yards
- 1988 Michigan Wolverines [9-2-1]
- 1988 Missouri Tigers [3-7-1] 5 players ran for over 242 yards
- 1988 Navy Midshipmen [3-8]
- 1988 Oklahoma Sooners [9-3] 6 players ran for over 308 yards

- 1989 Air Force Falcons [8-4-1] 3 players ran for over 703 yards
- 1989 Army Black Knights [6-5]
- 1989 Colorado Buffaloes [11-1] 6 players ran for over 213 yards
- 1989 Michigan Wolverines [10-2]
- 1989 Navy Midshipmen [3-8]
- 1989 Oklahoma Sooners [7-4]
- 1989 Yale Bulldogs [8-2]
- 1990 Air Force Falcons [7-5] 5 players ran for over 228 yards
- 1990 Army Black Knights [6-5]
- 1990 Colorado Buffaloes [11-1-1] 4 players ran for over 325 yards
- 1990 Oklahoma Sooners [8-3] 6 players ran for over 262 yards
- 1990 Yale Bulldogs [6-4]
- 1991 Air Force Falcons [10-3] 6 players ran for over 353 yards
- 1991 Army Black Knights [4-7]
- 1991 Colorado Buffaloes [8-3-1] 4 players ran for over 301 yards
- 1991 Yale Bulldogs [6-4]
- 1992 Air Force Falcons [7-5] 6 players ran for over 310 yards
- 1992 Army Black Knights [5-6]
- 1993 Air Force Falcons [4-8] 6 players ran for over 301 yards
- 1993 Army Black Knights [6-5]
- 1993 Oregon State Beavers [4-7] 5 players ran for over 338 yards
- 1994 Air Force Falcons [8-4] 6 players ran for over 435 yards
- 1994 Army Black Knights [4-7]
- 1994 Oregon State Beavers [4-7] 5 players ran for over 295 yards
- 1995 Army Black Knights [5-5-1]
- 1995 Oregon State Beavers [1-10] 6 players ran for over 251 yards
- 1996 Army Black Knights [10-2] 7 players ran for over 229 yards

- 1996 Oregon State Beavers [2-9] 4 players ran for over 387 yards
- 1997 Army Black Knights [4-7]
- 1998 Army Black Knights [3-8]
- 1999 Army Black Knights [3-8]

Honoring The Wishbone Boys - ALABAMA

- Keith Pugh
- Rick Neal
- John Turpin
- Randy Billingsley
- Ozzie Newsome
- John Crow
- Bruce Bolton
- Robert Frayley
- Willie Shelby
- Buddy Brown
- James Taylor
- Calvin Culliver
- Billy Jackson
- Jack O'Rear
- Lou Ikner
- Don Jacobs
- David Bailey
- Alan Gray
- Ken Coley
- Gary Rutledge
- Jeff Rutledge
- Richard Todd
- Kevin Jones
- John Hannah
- Johnny Musso
- Bill Davis
- Bucky Berry
- Alan McELroy
- Roger Chapman
- Walter Lewis
- Gary Elvis Britt
- Steve Whitman
- Lou Green
- Wilbur Jackson
- Johnny Davis
- Steadman Shealy

- Tony Nathan
- Thad Flanagan
- Jesse Bendross
- Jim Horton
- Wayne Reed
- Paul Spivey
- Steve Sprayberry
- David Knapp
- Steve Bisceglia
- Johnny Davis
- Barry McGee
- Philip Law
- Buddy Aydelette
- Terry Rowell
- Bobby McKinney
- Randy Hall
- James Sanderson
- Steve Mott
- Robin Cary
- Mike O'Toole
- Joe LaBue
- Allen Cox
- Jim Krapf
- Morris Hunt
- Vince Boothe
- Terry Davis
- Jim Simmons
- Warren Dyar
- James L White
- Ellis Beck
- Butch Ellard
- Michael Tucker
- Wayne Adkinson
- Rickey Gilliland
- Jack White
- Jay Vines
- Pat Raines
- Clay Moss
- Matthew "Scott" Allison

- Jimmy Rosser
- Ben Orcutt
- Tom McCrary
- Glenn Woodruff
- Mike Eckenrod
- Jim Bunch
- TB Nelson
- Joey Jones
- Ed Hines
- Dwight Stephenson
- Ron Richardson
- Johnny Dyess
- Major Ogilvie
- Billy Sexton
- Butch Hobson
- Benny Rippetoe
- Dexter Wood
- Randy Moore
- Pat Keever
- Fred Marshall
- Phil Murphy
- Pete Pappas
- Steve Patterson
- Sylvester Croom

Made in the USA
Middletown, DE
15 October 2020

22059132R00135